HAPPINESS,
IT'S YOUR CHOICE

Gary Applegate Ph.D

BERRINGER PUBLISHING
SHERMAN OAKS, CALIFORNIA

i

11 2833

15.00 10/86 Quality: City

Library of Congress Cataloging in Publication Data
Main entry under title:

Happiness, it's your choice.

Includes index.

Hard Cover   ISBN 0-9614987-0-6

Printed in the United States of America.

FOR SUZY

iii

CONTENTS

ACKNOWLEDGMENTS

This book was difficult to write and could not have been completed without the help of these caring, bright people:

Ed Ford and Jim Soldani gave the theoretical feedback to keep me on track.

Rhoda Greenstone contributed her extraordinary talents to organize and structure the development of the first draft.

Jim Lee, Bea Lumma, Yolanda Magnante, and Ina Potter patiently read the manuscript and gave their valuable comments that shaped the final draft.

Peggy Brown typed and re-typed, edited, and offered numerous helpful suggestions.

Pat Goehe took a sabbatical leave from Southern Illinois University and moved to Los Angeles. She enthusiastically devoted her time to the completion of this book. Her motivation and literary skills are tremendously appreciated.

Jim Benepe, M.D., my editor, would confess he didn't really understand the implication of saying he would help, but once he started, there was no stopping him. Thanks to Jim, my manuscript became immeasurably more clear and consistent.

Finally, my wife, Suzy, whose preciseness, encouragement, energy, and feedback were given unselfishly from start to finish. I am tremendously indebted to her . . . which means I'll be taking out the trash for a long time.

To all, I give my sincere thanks for helping write this book.

AUTHOR'S NOTE

I appreciate the lack of a universally acceptable, unigender personal pronoun. In hope of preserving a readable text, I have chosen to use "she" in some instances of universal statements and "he" in others. My intent is not to favor or discount either sex.

The case histories presented in this book are for instructional purposes. Names have been changed, and some cases represent a composite of several individuals.

I wish to extend my sincere appreciation to those who have granted me permission to tell their stories.

INTRODUCTION

Have there been times when you left a seminar or put a book down, decided to make plans to be different, and within a few days, lost your enthusiasm and gave up?

The advice that many dynamic speakers and accomplished authors give is inspirational. Yet, with all of this information, why do you return to old inefficient habits? What will it take, not only to start, but also to continue toward the kind of life-style you really want?

The answer is to discover another way, to develop a different strategy. To keep hitting your head against the same stone wall will only cause a headache, not a breakthough!

Happiness, It's Your Choice, is not just another how-to book to help people temporarily change what they are doing to feel better. It is a breakthrough for all people who want more power to feel good while living in a world which doesn't always give them what they want.

Successful change is a difficult process. Consider for a moment the following three questions. Do you change successfully when:

1. You first **think** you want to change?
2. You believe you can learn or you have the skills to **act**?
3. You decide that changing will be worth the effort because you will **feel** better?

If your answer is, "Yes, I will change when these three conditions are met," you agree that first thinking, then acting to feel better, is a natural process.

The Skill Development Theory integrates this natural process of changing what you think, to influence what you do, to feel happier, into a model that works in all environments. The model explains specific thinking and acting skills to more effectively deal with life's ongoing problems. With this new lifestyle, you will no longer be a victim, a procrastinator, or a manipulator. You won't be waiting for good days to happen. You will know, as I do now, how to make everyday a happy day!

PART I:
THE RETHINKING PROCESS

CHAPTER ONE

Where Most People Are

"If 'out there' would change, my
life would be better."

WhMPA

"I have never been able to conceive how any rational being
could propose happiness to
himself from the exercise of
power over others."

Thomas Jefferson

At 7:22 AM, October 22, 1978, I wrote in crayon on my bathroom mirror: "Everything I think and do is purposeful to meet my internal needs."

When this thought struck me, I knew I had begun to see the world differently. At that moment, I felt I had an edge, an insight that would give me a key to happiness. I knew I could gain control over my life as well as teach happiness to others. After many years as a therapist in private practice, I had learned from observation and personal experience that true joy occurs when a person has control over his own life. In the past I put myself in an out-of-control position by working to be an external problem-solver. You tell me your troubles; I lend you a sympathetic ear. I help you find plans to solve your problems, and we both find happiness. Right?

Wrong! Where I was then in my personal life, and where I believe most people are today, is believing that the problem is the spouse, the boss, the IRS, the kids, or a million other things in the outside world. For me professionally, the problem was my clients didn't always work productively to change. They wanted to change and even admitted what they had been doing wasn't always helping. I offered numerous plans, ingenious tools, and creative exercises, yet the rate of success was fifty-fifty. Some of my clients seemed to change, and the quality of their lives improved, but others kept going back to the same old troubles and habits.

Where Most People Are—WhMPA for short—can be described as a position that is neither weak nor strong. WhMPAs sometimes are happy, sometimes have success, but just as often, they are feeling out-of-control and puzzled about how to get people to give them what they want. They are usually working to be comfortable.

My journey of discovery began by recognizing how weak we feel when our happiness depends on "out there." If the WhMPA problems come from everyone and everything outside, and since we have no actual control over anyone or anything "out there," then the solution for living a better, happier life comes from **how I deal with the world and not how the world deals with me**. Think about it: Can we always make our employer treat us better, be less critical or less picky? Do we always have the ability to get a friend or mate to be more affectionate, be more cheerful, or less demanding? Can we correctly predict or control the stock market or the price of gold? Trying to take control of any of these is like trying to hold back a raging flood—we have very limited power over "out there." Yet WhMPAs expend an enormous amount of energy trying to get "out there" to change. "If only my boss would appreciate me, if only my spouse were more pleasant, if only my kids would behave, if only I could beat inflation, if only my client or friend weren't so depressed," are the WhMPA cries.

I have a confession. Many times, in those early days of my practice, I felt as helpless and frustrated as the WhMPAs who came to me for help. Although I offered practical solutions, I wasn't as successful in helping others as I wanted to be. Instead of asking them what they were thinking and what they really wanted, I would rush to give them a plan to change their actions. Soon I realized that standard psychological procedures were not enough. If people wanted a successful formula to deal with all their problems, and if I wanted to be an effective therapist and a happier person, I had to find a better way. Let me illustrate by an example of a man who was out-of-control and typified many of the problems of a WhMPA. Walt came to me overwhelmed with feelings of ineffectiveness at work and at home. He had all the trappings of success, yet he felt terribly overburdened. He held a management position with a prestigious firm. His wife, Cathy, worked as an escrow officer for a large bank, and they had three teenage children. At thirty-eight, Walt exercised regularly, appeared to be in good shape, and looked like a man capable of taking care of himself.

Yet Walt complained that he was exhausted, angry, and frustrated from taking care of everyone else's problems at work and at home. It was harder and harder for him to be on time for work every morning. Upon waking, there were chores to do, from feeding the kids and the dog, to policing the "new wave" fashions of his teenage children.

Walt told me how hard it was to constantly be cleaning up the mistakes and problems at the office, and then come home to one domestic crisis after another. All he wanted was some tranquility at home. Instead, Cathy greeted him with, "Jason's done it again. You'd better handle him!" or "Why didn't you pay the credit card bill?" or "There's something wrong with the dishwasher." When Walt came to me, I listened patiently to his extensive list of "problems." I was a caring, attentive listener. The mistake I made was allowing the entire focus of Walt's visits to be on his problem areas, giving heightened importance to only those aspects of his life. **Instead of looking at skills Walt could employ to improve the quality of his life**, I was reinforcing his negative perceptions.

"Well, Walt, what do you want to do about all these problems? For example, what can be done about being late to work?" In retrospect, I can see how foolish this approach was—here I was, the expert, asking the novice for advice. It was as if a man with a tumor went to a surgeon, and the surgeon asked him, "Well, what do you want to do, cut or not?" I soon realized that asking an out-of-control person how to gain control was not the best approach.

An alternative was to offer Walt an elaborate plan, so he could learn punctuality. With all the gusto of youth and with only good intentions, I focused on "the problem." I suggested that Walt put his alarm clock in the bathroom. That way he'd kill two birds with one stone—the amplified sound from the bathroom tiles would surely get him out of bed, and he'd be exactly where he needed to be to get started for the day. He could shower, brush his teeth, and be in the swing of it in no time.

Great plan? I thought so. Unfortunately, Walt didn't use it. Walt continued to arrive late to work. The "problem" wasn't the alarm clock, nor that Walt was too tired to get up in the morning. Who wouldn't resist going to a place where he felt exploited and got little, if any, recognition except when he made a mistake?

My next tactic was to get Walt to consider looking for another job. "Walt, why don't you start by getting in touch with an executive placement office or putting out feelers with some other company?" He began to get restless, shifting his body around and looking down at the floor. I made other suggestions such as looking in the papers, getting trade publication ads, asking business colleagues about openings elsewhere, and getting him to think of other resources.

The next time he came to my office I asked, "How did it go, Walt? Did you check the employment ads? Did you discuss possible openings with your colleagues?"

Walt's face got red, and he began rubbing the back of his neck. His eyes darted around the room. "Well, I thought about it. Oh, I did look in the paper, but there wasn't really anything for me. I have to say your idea about putting out feelers isn't a very good one. I mean, if word gets back to my boss, I could get fired! That's not a good idea at all."

With time, Walt only grew more miserable, felt more out-of-control, and more "trapped." I worried and thought about how Walt's misery could be alleviated. I decided that Walt could make things better at his present job since he wasn't working to find a new one.

The next time I saw Walt I asked, "What would make you happy at work? What could you change?"

At first Walt looked stymied, but then he brightened. "If my boss would just change how he treats me, I'd be fine. I mean, I'm a terrific worker. I've done a lot, gone out of my way to help. Even though I've contributed to this company, my boss, who is a vice-president, rarely seems to acknowledge what I do. I know if I could get him to notice the fine job I'm doing, everything would get better. How do you think it feels to have him call me into his office only when I make a mistake, or like yesterday, when I was late?"

"You mean after all this time you're still getting to work late?" I asked with noticeable irritation. Walt shrugged his shoulders and grinned.

So we went back to square one. Walt would put his alarm clock in the bathroom, and he would begin by getting to work on time. I then asked him to draw up a list of "do"s and "don't"s so he would be on the Vice-President's best side. We discussed his list, and he left my office with a plan to give his boss what he wanted. With this plan, both of us felt that his job would be more rewarding.

When Walt came back, he was dejected because the plan hadn't worked. "I gave up after a couple of days," he complained. "What's the use? The boss still criticized me! Why should I work hard to change what I'm doing when the results are still the same?"

My stress began to be as overwhelming as Walt's "problems." Out of frustration, I changed the subject and asked him how things were going at home. He despairingly replied, "I tried coming home with a joke or smile for Cathy, but the woman just nags and bosses. Doesn't she see that I just want a quiet hour to unwind?" He nervously tapped the arm of his chair; his other hand balled up in a fist. "She wants me to take care of this or that, or she sends the kids to me, 'Hey, Dad, you've got to help me with this problem.' I'll tell you, after a hard day at the office I just can't deal with them."

I questioned Walt about his relations with his children, trying to get him to think of some new ways to improve things. He replied, "I've really tried asking them how things were going. I even told them I'd take them on a fishing trip this year instead of going with my buddies. But that didn't work either. They were too busy with television or the phone or something." Bitterly Walt continued, "I guess things just aren't too good for me."

I was terribly frustrated that although Walt could adopt a change here or there, he couldn't consistently alter his behavior. Sure, he brought home a smile and a hug for his wife from time to time. He tossed the ball around with his kids or attempted to get involved in their lives. There were more times he was punctual at work, but all of the plans, exercises, methods, or motivational tapes I offered Walt were only temporary solutions.

I felt as though I had given Walt Band-Aids to put on gushing wounds! What he needed was basic information about how to live a better way. Walt really didn't need me to come up with "solutions." After all, he was capable of figuring out ways to get to work on time; there were other jobs available. He could be more involved with his kids, and he could be more pleasant to Cathy.

Walt needed a different **strategy**, a **new way** to deal with whatever stress came into his life. Temporary solutions were not the answer. Traditional therapy—where a professional is paid to listen, provide insight for their client, and suggest common sense actions to improve some situations—had only limited benefits.

How helpless Walt must have felt when he thought his happiness depended on his boss, his wife, or his kids changing. We feel great when we know we are running our own show. We don't feel so great when we see someone "out there" in the director's chair. It was foolish for Walt to try to change his actions to make his boss reward him. It was just as foolish for me to try to get Walt to change and be happy, so I would feel good about having helped him. We both needed a better way.

For the many Walts and Cathys of the world, just problem-solving wasn't the answer. After hundreds of seminars and questionnaires, and after my own personal journey of self-examination, certain truths emerged. The way for people to change from problem-solvers to Skill Builders must **begin** with thoughts. Walt had been asked to **act** differently, instead of taught how to **think** differently.

Becoming happy depends on rethinking such things as what we have control over, influence over, and what we cannot control. For example, how can we absolutley control our income, our family, and our future? If you recall Walt's "problems," he felt miserable because he could not make others do what he wanted. He was constantly thinking of tomorrow, pushing himself out of the present to some future happiness when he would get what he wanted. Even though I presented him with actions that let him know he had alternatives, Walt hung on to a job he hated and suffered through a poor relationship with all the members of his family. He believed he was "trapped," and consequently continued to be a victim of circumstances. Instead of beginning to take control by rethinking, Walt acted to change an environment over which he had little influence. His direction was that of a WhMPA. Does that necessarily make him a bad person?

Of course not. Walt, like each of us, was simply trying to meet his internal needs. He needed—the feeling of **security**, **faith** in himself, a sense of **self-worth**, to feel **free**, to **belong** and be loved, to have **fun**, to gain **knowledge** and feel **healthy**. These needs will be discussed in detail later. Everything Walt thought and did was an attempt to get his needs met. Because his thinking was not focused on his immediate need, his actions got him what he needed only now and then.

Looking back, I now know that when Walt wanted his boss's approval at work, what he needed was an effective way to satisfy his need for worth. In trying to get approval, he gave away control over his life to his boss as well as to his wife and children. He thought he "had to" go to work; he "had to" solve everyone's problems. Small wonder he felt trapped! He met his freedom need one week of the year on a fishing trip with his buddies. The remaining fifty-one weeks were spent running from stress, feeling coerced into a life he didn't enjoy. Walt was into outcome, not process. He didn't see many choices. In trying to control "out there" he lost control for himself.

What if Walt had options? In fact, what if all of us could think of many alternatives to get our needs met? An effective **strategy** to fulfill our needs is now available to all who choose to use it. It **begins** by learning how to **evaluate** your world and then to **rethink** in the following five areas:

1. DISCOVERING WHAT WE CAN CONTROL. RETHINKING FROM "OUT THERE" TO "ME."

2. RETHINKING FROM A WANT LEVEL TO A NEED LEVEL FOR FULFILLMENT.

3. GIVING UP OUR NOTIONS OF BEING FORCED, COMPELLED, OR VICTIMIZED, TO RETHINKING THAT WE HAVE CHOICES.

4. MOVING FROM OUTCOME AND LEARNING TO ALSO ENJOY THE PROCESS.

5. RETHINKING THAT STRESS, THE DIFFERENCE BETWEEN WHAT WE WANT AND WHAT WE HAVE, IS NOT ALWAYS TO BE FEARED. IT CAN BE AN OPPORTUNITY TO HELP US GROW.

I have conducted training seminars for thousands of people. When I have asked the question, "What are we all working for?" the answer has always been, "To feel good and be happy." You and I may use different ways, but we all have the same goal. When I looked at those different ways, I saw that some of us had more success. What worked for me was to take these areas of rethinking and practice them until I changed my way of viewing the world.

Picture a person who feels terrific and exudes happiness. This person is secure; he* has skills to get the things he wants. You can see how much he believes in himself. His posture tells you he is thinking, "I can do it!" He achieves something every day because he risks something each day, and he is always growing beyond where he was yesterday. This is not a person who feels he is stuck in his job or trapped in his marriage; he is a person who knows he has many choices. He feels confident around people, whether they are business associates or social acquaintances. He sees himself as someone who can make fun happen. He doesn't feel locked into a lifestyle. He doesn't wait for good things to happen. This person finds interesting, enjoyable, fun things to do—from trying a new exotic restaurant, to telling a joke, to smiling at a stranger. He is constantly putting new experiences and information into his life. This is a person who creates a balance between his physiological and psychological health. Would you like to be this person?

Consider the quality of your life if you had unlimited choices for happiness and if you had control over feeling good. Would you hate feeling at ease around people? Would it be awful to be a fun-maker? If you're like me, I suspect you'd enjoy being balanced, happy, and healthy. The next five chapters will teach you how to **evaluate** what you are doing and to **rethink**, to start you on your own journey of well-being. I want to teach you the skills, **the strategy, to make your life the happiest it can possibly be**. Are you ready?

---

*With respect to the use of personal pronouns in the text, I have attempted to alternate genders. (See Author's Note.)

CHAPTER TWO

What I Can Control

"I can't help the way I think."

WhMPA

"The highest possible stage in
moral culture is when we recognize that we ought to control our
thoughts."

C. Darwin

Last summer my wife, Suzy, and I toured the Southwest United States, concluding the trip with a visit to my cousin, Wendy, in Phoenix. Three months earlier, she had her first child, a beautiful seven pound, ten ounce boy. She asked me to be the baby's godfather, and the christening took place during our visit. I was excited, honored, and curious. This was a new role for me!

The baptism was held at a large, historic cathedral, with all the traditional rituals of candles, incense, robes, and oils associated with the Catholic Church. It was going to be a great day!

What happened was not exactly what godfather Gary expected. All the leading characters were on time except for the priest. It was August and very hot, and the air conditioning wasn't working properly. The baby was upset and started to cry. Had I not worried about looking foolish, I might have cried too.

Wendy, a wonderful caring person, tried to comfort the baby by feeding him, holding him, talking to him, and everything else most new mothers do in that situation. I remember thinking this was all very normal. Finally the priest arrived, apologizing for his delay. Now it was my turn to hold the baby, get him to stop crying, and "listen up" for this most important experience in his young life! As I took the child, instead of listening up, he threw up, all over my brand new summer suit. What a mess! My coat, tie, pants, and even my shoes had been baptized! Quite a memorable day! I wouldn't exactly call it a "10," but I'd have to call it memorable.

I am sure you can guess the problem. The baby was too warm and uncomfortable. He was crying to communicate that he was miserable. His reward was formula, which he did not want. He proceeded to let all of us know that—in what I felt to be a most inappropriate manner. Certainly one would think that adults could have a situation like that under their control!

Over the years, I recall many parents who came to me wanting their children to act differently, as I had with my godchild. In the past, I gave my clients action plans, as I did with Walt in the previous chapter, to help them get what they wanted. Today I realize that was a foolish starting point. In fact, it was one hundred and eighty degrees in the wrong direction. When you punish and/or reward, you are usually thinking, "I want to change what some other person is doing so that I can feel better."

I don't know the exact point in development when people work to change what others think, do, and feel, but I suspect this focus on "out there" has a lot to do with the way we get our needs met as infants. For many of us, the first and only way to gain control over the environment is by crying. Through crying, an infant usually gets an adult to meet his needs. When an infant cries, others respond to what the baby is feeling, as Wendy did, in order to give the child what it needed. Therefore, from the very beginning of our lives, we develop habits which effect change in others or our environment. It works quite well when others perceive us as helpless. Could you imagine not attending to a crying child who is hungry or wet? As adults, to maximize our influence over others, we can appear helpless or powerful. I believe we pay a tremendous price with either position. There is an alternative which will get us even more of what we want. The alternative is to first **evaluate what we want or need and compare it to what we have**. When we interpret a difference—with my godchild I wanted quiet and clean; I had crying and messy— we'll feel stress. The stress motivates us to do something. We can choose to react or rethink. WhMPAs react; Skill Builders rethink.

Rethinking is a process whereby we change our interpretations of the world. With rethinking, we can ask ourselves: **What do we control? What do we really need? What are our choices? Are we in process? Can we benefit from this moment?** If we can rethink and change our interpretations about what we are perceiving, we can then set priorities to act to achieve more happiness.

The next page illustrates a familiar cartoon of two people looking at a glass of water. It's the same glass, yet one person sees (perceives) it as half empty while the other views it as half full. The glass is the same; the **interpretations** are different. We don't always realize that we have choices over how we perceive our world, in this instance, a glass of water. Given a choice, would you want your glass half full or half empty?

OUR PERCEPTIONS CONTROL
WHAT WE DO

When dealing with parents in the last several years, I have asked pointed questions to help them understand the process of rethinking their perceptions of the environment before they act. Questions like, what do they have control over when it comes to raising their children? When I teach parents they don't have total control over what their children do, even if their child is only three months old, they start to perceive their children differently. If I can get parents to accept that what they really have control over is what they, themselves, think and do, then I have succeeded.

When WhMPAs think about reducing stress, they usually react by trying to change something "out there" to agree with them. Of course, being human and living in a socialized world, we are all influenced by others. The problem arises when we try to control others rather than our perceptions of them. Controlling others leads to all kinds of frustrations since what we do to them rarely elicits the specific response we want. People do not behave in an entirely consistent manner, and we can't predict what goes on in their heads. Most people know they can't always influence others, yet because they are successful some of the time, they never stop trying.

If I had taken the time to teach Walt how to **rethink** what he could control, influence, or could not control, he would have thought, acted, and felt differently. He would have perceived his boss, wife, and children as people he could sometimes influence, not control in such a way as to get what he wanted. He certainly would not have worked on a plan to get his boss to notice how good his performance was at work. What control did he have over the boss noticing, and even if he did, reacting in a positive manner? Who can say for certain under what agenda Walt's boss might be functioning for his own need fulfillment?

You might wonder what you have control over each day. Rethink: Can you **demonstrate caring** towards others even if they do things that are different from what you want? The answer is "yes" if you **interpret** your need fulfillment as not dependent exclusively on what they do. The answer is "no" if you believe your happiness depends on their caring, and they don't. If you want them to care and they don't, you will feel rejected, hurt, and probably say, "To hell with you!" You'll move away because you need something different from what you received. If you are thinking, "I can only change me, and I have complete control over saying 'hello', giving a compliment, smiling, listening, giving a hug," you will approach first.

Can you **ask questions** that allow for many answers, give others ideas, and avoid criticizing? Can you rethink that what you have control over is your **question** and not their **answer**?

Can you **give alternatives** to help others with their lives? What if they don't react positively to your information? When you want people to change and they don't, you will be frustrated. If that happens too often, you will move away and stop sharing your ideas. Do you move away because you want something you really have no control over getting?

Wherever you are, can you share and **model self-controlling thoughts and actions**? If others perceive you as happy, and Skill Building to be happier, might they be **more** influenced by what you think and do?

To summarize, you can rethink your perceptions of your relationships to: caring, asking questions, giving alternatives, and modeling strong behavior regardless of what others might do.

By rethinking, you will discover new perceptions that will give you more control in dealing with others. Remember, **it begins with changing what you think of your world**. To demonstrate how powerful thoughts are, imagine that when you go to bed Friday night, you think of waking up to a sunny day so you and a friend can go on a picnic. When you wake up on Saturday, the sky is cloudy, and there is a strong, cold wind. There is a big difference between the picture in your head, your expectations, and what you perceive. I call that difference "frustration" or "stress." Most people call that difference "a problem." You might **think** that because there is a big difference between the thought in your head and the environment, you have to react to the situation by feeling badly. Would you feel depression, anger, or self-pity in such a situation? Would you call your friend to complain, put off the picnic until it was sunny, and continue to "ruin" the day with negative feelings?

If you can rethink first, you will see you have the **choice** between letting habitual behavior take over or selecting new interpretations to meet your needs in a more efficient way. If you rethink to meet the challenge of the frustration, you will consider what you can and cannot control. Can you control the weather? No way! Can you influence your friend into doing something else? Maybe! Can you ask her to play racquetball, go to the movies, or come over and play Gin Rummy? Absolutely! If she says "no," could you call some other friends and offer your suggestions for spending time together on a rainy cold day?

You have total control over being friendly (she didn't

change the weather), thinking of ideas, asking questions, giving alternatives, and being enthusiastic about what the day has to offer. You only have some influence with her and no control over making it warm and sunny.

Are you convinced how important your thinking is in determining what you can control? Understanding that human behavior comprises a package made up of thoughts, actions, and feelings will help in your rethinking. Each component influences the others, but if you want to be a **Skill Builder, your thoughts precede your actions or feelings**.

Imagine that human behavior is a triangle—thoughts are one mode, actions another, and feelings a third.

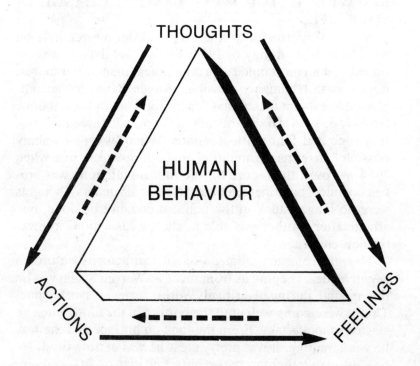

By allowing feelings or actions to come first, we lose control over our interpretation of what we are perceiving. Although there are some people who believe they have no choices, they are choosing one mode of behavior over others in everything they do. Skill Building teaches us that frustration is the initial response when "out there," what we perceive, is different from the thought we have, what we need. The initial thought of not being able to go on a picnic produces a negative, painful feeling. First comes this momentary frustration, and then we choose one of three modes of behavior. We can choose to continue to feel badly, act impulsively, or we can choose to think through our options. If we choose to evaluate, and then **rethink** our interpretation of the situation, we have increased the possibility for happiness and success by learning skills we can carry into every situation.

THOUGHT IS THE MOST POWERFUL MODE OF BEHAVIOR IF YOU WANT LASTING CHANGE IN YOUR LIFE.

In case you are still a little skeptical, let me remind you what happened on May 6, 1954. Before that date, it was assumed that no one could run a mile in less than four minutes; it just wasn't humanly possible. Roger Bannister accomplished a feat that tossed that "fact" right out of the window. On May 6, 1954, Dr. Bannister ran the mile in three minutes, fifty-nine and four-tenths seconds. What "wasn't humanly possible" in terms of running changed forever, because when 1954 was over, the record for the four-minute mile was broken not once, but nineteen times! Now that runners' thoughts were no longer stuck in the belief it couldn't be done, one athlete after another was able to change his actions to meet the new challenge.

Thought has such great power; it can actually enforce a negative idea, keeping us from success. Warren Spahn was on the mound during a critical World Series playoff game. Things were going well until the bottom of the ninth when he started to look shaky. From the look on his face and the way he was straining, it was pretty clear he was getting tired. He was ahead 4-2; there were two outs, and men on first and second. Warren was really struggling.

The manager came out of the dug-out, called time out and approached the pitcher. "You think you can handle it?" the manager asked. "Think you can get this guy out?"

The batter, Elston Howard, a real home-run hitter, was a

threat at any time, and especially in this kind of pressure situation. The pitcher looked at the batter, then down at the ground. "Yeah, I can do it," he answered, shuffling his foot on the mound.

"Listen," the manager said in a confidential whisper, "whatever you do, don't throw a high and outside pitch to this guy. That's his pitch for a home run. Got me? Don't throw it high and outside."

The manager turned around and left. What do you think the pitcher threw? A high and outside pitch! Elston parked it, and the game was over.

The manager left the pitcher with a dominant thought that determined his actions. If the manager had said, "Be sure and throw low and inside," maybe he would have done what he intended. But the dominant thought was "high and outside," which was reinforced twice by the manager—and high and outside was all he could throw. You can see how thought controlled actions here, changing the thought in the pitcher's mind so that he lost the game.

Maybe you can identify with Warren Spahn if you've ever been in a pressure situation. Take the first hole of a golf game, with your friends standing around, watching your performance while they are waiting to tee off. You know the right is out-of-bounds, so you think, "Whatever I do, don't hit it right."

Just before you hit, your "friend," and opponent for the day, comes up to you and jokingly says, "Careful, Fred! The right side is out-of-bounds!"

You know it's a psych job, but the thought has now been reinforced. If you don't visualize your best swing and the ball traveling two hundred and twenty yards down the left middle of the fairway, what will undoubtedly happen will be one of two alternatives—both horrible! You swing too hard and too fast, arms first, slicing the ball out-of-bounds, or you overcompensate so much that you don't hit the ball squarely, and it flies three inches above the ground, "a worm warmer," for fifty yards ahead left. Of course your friends say nothing. What can be said to someone whose dominant thought was what **not** to do, instead of what **to do**?

I hope you now understand that a thought, positive or negative, can control your actions. Your actions and thoughts then determine how you feel. If you want more good feelings, it is imperative that you rethink your interpretations of the world. By changing what is coming in you can more easily change what is going out to be happier.

When you are in-control, you think, "If only **I** would change, I would feel better," rather than, "If only my spouse/boss/friend/" 'out there' would change, I would feel better."

With this information stored in your brain forever, it's time to act. A good positive step is to write out three personal lists. The first list will be those things you have **control over**, and it might look something like this:

WHAT I CAN CONTROL

How I have fun
What I say
Changing the picture in
   my head
How positive my attitude is
How often I exercise
What I eat or drink
What I think of myself
How long I feel bad
Giving a compliment
What I buy, and how much
   I spend
Getting organized

Alternatives I give to others
Which books I read
When I smile and say hello
Applying for a job
How much television I watch
What I think of others
What risks I take
How I dress
Writing a letter
Dialing a phone number
Learning a new skill
Owning a pet
What time I go to bed

What can you add to this list?

_____   _____

_____   _____

_____   _____

WHAT I CAN INFLUENCE

Winning a game of skill
Getting others to buy my
    product or service
How my pet behaves
Local government
Getting my child to eat
Personal finances
Getting a raise

Being on time
My environment
What people close to me
    might do
Stopping my child from
    crying
How I might die

What can you add to this list?

_____   _____

_____   _____

_____   _____

The third list will include those things over which you have absolutely **no control**.

WHAT I CANNOT CONTROL

Weather
What my team does on
    television
Birth defects due to genetic
    causes

Living forever
The past
What strangers may do
My plane landing on time
The passing of time

What can you add to this list?

_____   _____

_____   _____

_____   _____

If your three lists compare to mine, what you can control is longer than the list of what you can influence. The list of what you cannot control is the shortest. Isn't that comforting? My suspicions are what you cannot control will stay constant. As a Skill Builder, you have infinite choices to gain more control of what you take in and what you put out. What you can't control is finite, and what you have influence over is understood as just that—influence.

WhMPAs approach life mostly from an **action** and **feeling** perspective; a Skill Builder changes his life by first choosing **thought**. When action is the focal point of your behavior, your life could be like Walt's, back at the beginning of my practice. Walt's actions gave him limited success, a kind of hit-or-miss fulfillment of his needs. Taking the time to evaluate and rethink can take us from out-of-control to in-control, so we have unlimited choices about our lives. Even though old habits of working to change others may sometimes serve us, they are usually inefficient. In the next chapter, a second area to rethink will give you a choice to take control to get more of what you **really** need.

CHAPTER THREE

Moving From What You WANT
To What You NEED

"I want what I want when I want it."

WhMPA

"You can't always get what you want, but if you try sometimes, you just might find, you get what you need."

The Rolling Stones

You and I are on an airplane. The plane lands for a stopover before we complete the last leg of our journey. The pilot announces there will be a fifty minute period before we take off. He says there is enough time to get off the plane and stretch our legs, but be sure to take along our boarding passes.

We are so engrossed in conversation, before we know it, only you and I and the man in front of us are left on the plane. The pilot steps up to the man and asks him if he would like some assistance to take a walk. The gentleman, who is blind, indicates that he would like to stay, but suggests to the pilot that his seeing eye dog would like some exercise. The pilot takes the dog and follows us into the terminal.

When it comes time to reboard, you and I get into the crowd of fellow passengers milling around, impatient to be back in the air.

Along comes the pilot, wearing wrap-around sunglasses, being pulled roughly by this strange seeing eye dog. "I've heard of instrument flying," one of the passengers shouts, "but this is ridiculous!" Some people's mouths drop; some look very worried. Several are so upset, they insist the pilot take off the glasses and show them he has perfect eyesight before they will get back on the plane. You and I have been aware of the facts from the beginning, so we merely chuckle over the comedy of errors.

What happened in this fun story? You and I saw the same thing as the other passengers, but we had information they didn't have. **That information gave us a perception which enabled us to maintain a balance many of them could not keep.** We had no reason for fear, confusion, worry, or anxiety because we had a different interpretation of what was happening.

When we have information that gives us alternatives to meet our needs, it helps us gain confidence. It is the difference between feeling at the mercy of fate and feeling in-control of what is happening. When we develop skills— **new ways to think and act to meet our needs**—we are in the process of living successful lives and gaining the feeling of fulfillment.

Remember, **everything we think and do is directed to meet our internal needs.** The degree and method of need fulfillment varies, due to genetic differences and environmental background. For example, you were raised by a family who expressed love through hugs and kisses. Your spouse was raised with caring words and very little touching. Although you both have a need for love/belonging, you have learned different ways to express it.

I believe we have eight internal needs. Suzy feels there is a ninth need . . . CHOCOLATE!!! I think she's teasing, but at times I'm not sure. Some may believe there are more, others less. Regardless, what is important is that all thoughts and actions are purposeful, directed to meet our internal needs. Therefore, an essential step to taking control over our lives is to begin by identifying those needs: **SECURITY, FAITH, WORTH, FREEDOM, BELONGING, FUN, KNOWLEDGE, and HEALTH**.

1. SECURITY:

I feel secure when I have skills to efficiently meet all my needs. I also feel secure when I have a sense of personal strength, when I have **control** over my life, when I realize I can't control what anyone else does or thinks.

Example: I'm scheduled to speak before a large audience. I could worry about how they'll react to me, whether or not they'll like me, and accept what I say. I could also put to use all my skills in preparing as best I can, rehearsing with friends, and making my speech as effective as possible. I can't control the audience response, but I can feel secure about the process I use to build my speech composition and delivery skills.

2. FAITH:

Faith is a **belief** in me to meet my needs to be happy, as well as a belief in a greater power. Faith is a positive attitude about myself and life in general.

Example: We all know of individuals or teams being told they have no chance of succeeding, and the next thing you know, they defy all the odds and accomplish the impossible. The U.S. Olympic Hockey Team of 1980, Susan B. Anthony, working against tremendous odds for women's suffrage, and Joe Kennedy, skiing with only one leg—these people all **believed** they could grow and succeed in meeting their needs.

3. WORTH:

When I sense a positive value about myself, see that I have gone a step beyond where I was, I feel worth. Through action and risk-taking, I feel good because I am **achieving**.

Example: I am seeking new information by attending a class; I realize I have been sitting in the back of the room, only answering questions when I've been called on. When I seat myself up front, make myself visible, and volunteer by raising my hand, I have risked and feel I've grown as a person. I feel worth.

4. FREEDOM:

Freedom is a state of mind, not a condition of the environment. It comes from knowing we have **choices** over what we think and do. I feel free when I rethink, rather than when I merely react or wait for things to happen. Freedom is an exhilarating feeling that comes from responsible behavior.

Example: Walt felt he was "trapped" in a job where he was exploited and unappreciated. Was Walt free to refuse to go to a job he hated everyday? Was Walt free to look for another job? Because he thought he had no choices, he became the victim of circumstances. Similarly, because he couldn't see options with his wife and children, his relationship with them continued to deteriorate. Walt was not free because he had limited himself by expecting others to change.

5. BELONGING /LOVE:

I feel I belong when I have friends, when I am involved in community activities, and when I care for others. I am demonstrating love when I put others first. The beginning of the process of love is **commitment**.

Example: A friend excitedly called to tell me he had tickets for the World Series. I was thrilled. Suzy asked what all the excitement was about. Since she is a baseball fan, I expected her to be happy for me. Instead she looked terribly disappointed. I asked what was wrong, and she reminded me the tickets were for the same night as her parents' thirty-fifth wedding anniversary party. My friend could always get someone else to go. I kept my commitment to the party. I satisfied all my needs by choosing Suzy and her parents over the Series.

6. FUN /ENJOYMENT:
When I experience laughter, excitement, humor at work, home, or anywhere, I am having fun. When I **make fun happen** I feel a special joy of accomplishment that only a sense of humor can bring.

Example: To see the fun side, to appreciate the ridiculous, and to laugh at our troubles is one of the greatest skills we can develop. A friend of mine took a risk and went windsurfing for the first time last week. I asked him how he liked it. "I am so sore I can hardly move! Boy, it's great but hard work!" he said. "It looked so easy, but I did nothing but fall. Everytime I fell, the people on the beach laughed. They did a lot of laughing, and so did I! It was so much fun!"

7. KNOWLEDGE:
The more information I gain, the more **alternatives** I have, the closer I come to achieving need fulfillment.

Example: Suzy and I went to Hawaii. Upon arrival, I had severe pain in my groin. I feared I had a hernia, an operation was in order, my vacation was ruined, and the pain would only get worse. Some vacation! After a miserable first day, Suzy convinced me to see a doctor. Reluctantly, I limped my paining body over for an exam. It was no hernia—just a pulled muscle. After rest and a muscle relaxant, I'd be fine. With that knowledge, my perceptions changed tremendously, and so did my vacation.

8. HEALTH:
When there is a **balance** between my physiological and psychological needs, I feel healthy. When I feel unhealthy, it is a direct signal to change what I am thinking about the world around me.

Example: Do you know someone who jogs for several miles each morning or works out strenuously, but seems rigid in his outlook on life and criticizes others for being weak? When we take care to exercise and put healthful food into our bodies, then sacrifice the need to belong, to get worth, by unduly criticizing people who eat junk food, we are not really taking care of ourselves efficiently. Health is a balance of all our needs.

There are different ways to meet these internal needs. Each of us have learned alternatives that we call **wants**. We may **want** money, a shapely body, a relationship, a new car, popularity, an evening out, fast service, or good luck.

To understand your wants better, think of yourself as a large wagon with eight spoke wheels, four on each side. Each wheel has a center part or hub, and spokes which support the wheel much like a bicycle wheel.

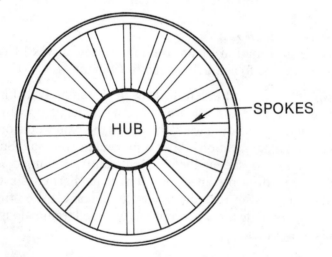

On one side, you have four wheels which bear the words **SECURITY, FAITH, WORTH, and FREEDOM** on their hubs. On the other side, the four wheels bear the words **BELONGING, FUN, KNOWLEDGE, and HEALTH**.

What is it that supports the wagon and keeps the wheels from bending or collapsing? Spokes. In terms of Skill Building, those spokes represent our **wants**. If you can think

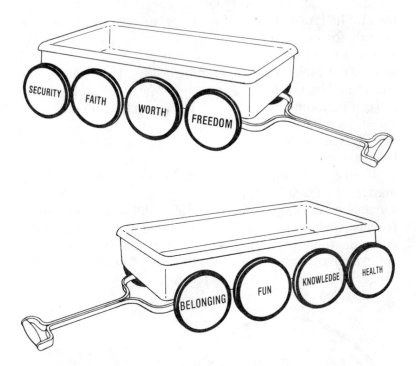

of **wants** as choices, options, pathways, or alternatives available to us to meet our needs, it might help you recognize the importance of opening your mind to as many possibilities as you can conceive.

Imagine having only one friend or spoke for your belonging wheel. Over the years I have seen many clients who had very few pathways or "spokes" to meet their different needs.

Annie was twenty-eight, five feet eleven inches, with long brown hair, high cheek bones, a thin model-like figure, and the saddest brown eyes I had ever seen. She was a total contradiction to her inward insecurity and inability to meet her needs, especially in the belonging area.

In our first meeting, she blurted out she was terribly lonely, felt ugly, and unwanted. That was difficult for me to believe from my first visual impression. She told me her story of how she had been, for the last six years, with David, a very successful Beverly Hills attorney. She loved him so much that she quit her job to be available whenever David wanted to travel. She moved into his townhouse and depended on him entirely for support. She stopped seeing most of her friends and in fact, did very little each day except care for David. She **wanted** to be married to him for the last five years and finally confronted him with the ultimatum, "Marry me, or let me go so I can find someone else." He chose to end the relationship, and she was devastated. She couldn't believe he did not want her. She had been depressed, angry, and even suicidal for the last two months.

When I asked what she wanted, her only reply was to be married to David. Annie was working on one precarious spoke to meet her need for belonging. She stayed away from friends, was unaware when men looked at her, and wasn't doing anything to put herself in an environment where she could meet new people. She was thinking, "I **want** David and if I can't have him, I'll be unhappy forever."

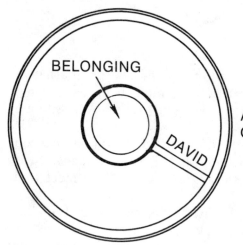

ANNIE'S WHEEL:
ONE SPOKE/DAVID

Certainly David was a pathway for Annie to meet her need for belonging and even fun, knowledge, and security, but was he the only pathway?

I began to teach Annie how to rethink from a **want level, where the answer to her problem was involvement with**

David, to a need level, where she saw that what she was really losing was belonging. David was one way to get belonging, but not the only way. Because Annie limited herself to only one spoke or want in her belonging wheel, when David pulled out, she was left with a broken wheel as well as a "broken heart."

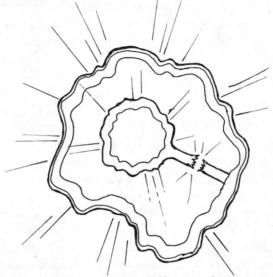

Annie eventually learned the difference between what she wanted—David, and what she **really needed**—belonging. When she started to rethink on a need level, she was able to meet other people, start working again, and accept that life without David could be happy. **She moved from what she couldn't control—David, to what she could control—the satisfaction of her need for belonging**. Annie became more flexible, not just in her actions, but also in her thoughts. This change was gradual not temporary, and would affect her life positively in all future relationships.

Realizing that **wants** are all the choices we select to meet our needs gives us greater flexibility to change what we can control. One pathway by itself should never be that terribly important. The idea is to have as many skills and choices as possible, so we don't depend upon a single want, as Annie did, for happiness. That doesn't mean we can't have special, intimate relationships. Rethinking that people are pathways, and that at any time we can lose a person through death, divorce, children growing up and leaving, or friends moving away, puts us at a need level. It is important to rethink that we are in-control of starting new pathways if old wants are no longer available.

Are the needs in a hierarchy of importance? Not really. The most important need in my life is that particular need or needs which are unfulfilled at that moment. For example, I may be achieving wonderfully in my career, yet feel no sense of belonging. I may have friends and family around me, yet my health is poor. The need area lacking at any given time should be the one on which to concentrate. Unfortunately, sometimes we overachieve in an area in which we feel secure, rather than risk fulfillment in other needs to get balance.

There are also times when our lives are going well except for one area. Clint, a good friend of mine, enjoyed his job, loved his children, wife, home, and was optimistic about his future. Everything was positive except when he and his wife disagreed, and the solution called for a compromise. This didn't happen often, but when it did, Clint lost belonging. Since he was a strong Skill Builder, the rest of his life was fine. It was mainly belonging with his wife that suffered. Why wasn't he able to compromise and give to someone he truly cared about?

Compromising is easy to suggest, but I believe very difficult to do. I also believe it won't work continuously if you don't see yourself meeting enough of your needs. Giving in can be very rewarding since it usually increases belonging. If, however, you feel a great loss in self-worth or fun, you won't always choose giving in.

As I discuss in the chapter on Belonging, two people stay together for mutual need fulfillment. If one person **wants** to go to the beach for a weekend and the other **wants** to go to a mountain cabin, one will have to sacrifice what they want. Clint found himself in this very situation. He wanted to go to the beach and spend time at the zoo in San Diego. His wife, Diane, hated zoos, but was excited about spending time with two other couples and their children in a mountain cabin at Lake Arrowhead. Time for a compromise you say. Fine, if either Clint or Diane is willing to go to the other person's location. However, if each dislikes the other's choice, feels he or she has given enough lately and wants the control of choosing, there will be problems.

The solution to Clint and Diane's conflict is not easy, but solvable if both will take a moment and rethink what they **really need**. They need to feel fulfillment. If they feel forced or controlled, then changing in a compromising direction won't be a strong possibility. Thoughts like, "I can't have fun at the other person's place," or "I don't even like you at this moment, why should I give in?" will make the problem worse.

To change actions you first change thoughts. You want control? You need worth. You want the beach? You need fun. You want peace and cooperation? You need belonging. If you can't get exactly what you want, are you able to change your thoughts about your partner and still get what you need? Is it possible to view her as working to meet her needs? Can you see her as needing worth, fun, and belonging, instead of control, the beach, and cooperation? With a different interpretation of why she is acting this way, can you change what you do? By also rethinking that giving is under your control, that it is an alternative to taking, and it increases worth, belonging, and fun, you are changing your thoughts, and the act of compromise is not so difficult. When Clint and Diane think that what they are both doing is need fulfilling, then compromising—selecting a third place, a day at each place, or going to the other's place this time and reversing it the next time—will be possible.

Thinking on a need level will help you understand that you have many choices, and the world is not a place where every stimulus produces a set response. When the alarm clock goes off in the morning, do you always jump right out of bed? When you see a coin on the sidewalk, do you always stop to pick it up? When people say "Hi," do you always say "Hi" back? **Remember your action will depend upon your interpretation of what you perceive**.

Do you have a choice to evaluate a difference between what you need and what you have? By rethinking from a want to a need level, your actions will be programmed to directly meet needs. Will having your needs met give you happiness right now?

CHAPTER FOUR

Choosing Our Thoughts, Actions, and Feelings

"You made me love you, I didn't want to do it."

WhMPA

"There is a positive side, and a negative side; at each moment you decide."

Bernard Gunther

Each day all of us make both efficient and inefficient choices to meet our psychological needs. Predictably, those inefficient alternatives we choose result in our feeling weak and out-of-control. Efficient choices which meet our needs make us feel strong and in-control of our lives. The pathways, or wants we select to meet our needs, are different for each of us. There is no set of pathways carved in stone which can meet everyone's needs in the same way all the time. For example, coffee at 8 AM may be stimulating, whereas at 11:30 PM, it may inhibit sleep. "Sleeping over" may be wonderful if the next morning is open, but not so great if you have a 7 AM appointment. You will make your own value judgment regarding those wants that give you positive feelings and those wants that don't give enough. I wouldn't really want to meet any needs by skydiving, yet you might choose skydiving for worth, fun, knowledge, belonging, faith, and even—my poor stomach—health! If your instructor throws the report you worked on all weekend into the waste basket, would you successfully be meeting your needs by jumping up and down, waving your arms, and turning colors? I think not. But if your child runs into the street, waving your arms, jumping up and down, yelling, and turning colors might be very effective.

There are efficient and inefficient choices. You decide if your thoughts and actions are an efficient choice by reviewing the consequences of what you are doing. Below I have listed **consequences** of your choice.

Inefficient Choice Consequences	**Efficient Choice Consequences**
1. Meet one of more of the eight needs.*	1. Meet one or more of the eight needs.*
2. **But** create or frustrate other needs. (Pay negative prices.)	2. No loss of fulfillment in other needs.

*All behavior, whether inefficient or efficient, is purposeful to meet our needs.

3. Feel out-of-control because you are trying to change other people, things, or situations.

4. Trying to change the past or control the future.

5. Going impatiently for immediate payoff. (Outcome.)

6. Feel comfortable.

3. Feel in-control because you are changing self, not others.

4. Working in the present or planning (creating options) for the future. (Process.)

5. Immediate payoff is power, mastery, and control of your life.

6. Feel fulfilled.

If you perceive comfortable (little or no stress) as a desirable state, then you may choose inefficient pathways to meet your needs. That may sound strange, but I believe you won't take too many risks when you perceive stress as something to be feared and avoided. Comfortable is maintaining the status quo and working for gratification by using only established habits. Staying in a safe but boring job, making few new friends, watching hours of television for fun, and doing the same things day after day give some people comfort. Being comfortable is not necessarily acting lazy, irresponsible, or unusual. For WhMPAs, it is the best way to meet their needs. It is inefficient because there is little growth. Taking a risk to build skills, whether stressed or not, is the joy of life. The consequence is a feeling of fulfillment which is a far better feeling than comfortable. It's your choice!

Have you ever felt that destiny rules your life—that you really have no choices because of how you were programmed as a child or because of your handicaps? Do you feel forced, compelled, or coerced into doing something against your will? Are you a victim? Have you played that role?

If you answered "yes," you have felt pain. Being a victim could give some happiness, but we pay great prices. If you think you didn't make choices in such circumstances, I assure you that you did.

Do you recall the old Jack Benny routine in which a guy jumps out, sticks a gun in Benny's ribs, and shouts, "Your money or your life!" Benny slaps his hand to his face, staring at the audience. The bandit pokes Benny in exasperation. "Buddy, you deaf or something? I said, 'your money or your life!'"

Benny whimpers, "I'm thinking! I'm thinking!" Now the bandit grabs Benny by the collar. "Okay, okay," Benny whines, "take my life—I'll need the money for the funeral."

We laugh because we know that Benny had a choice, and the pathway he took is ridiculous. For most of us, the choice between losing our money or losing our lives is obvious. However, we don't always have that clear-cut view of the choices we make if we feel victimized. That helpless feeling is alleviated through **rethinking** that we make choices in how we interpret and then act upon the environment.

Think for a moment, what are your choices? Do you choose your interpretations of what you perceive? Picture two people watching the same football game on television. One person is angry, the other happy. How is that possible? When you realize that stress or happiness is not what is occurring in the environment, but **your interpretation**, you begin to gain an edge in controlling your perceptions. Epictetus, in the first century A.D., may have anticipated our Super Bowl reactions when he said, "People are disturbed, not by things, but by the views they take of them."

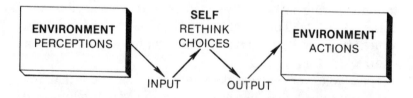

You can choose your input perceptions and your output actions. By rethinking control/influence/no-control, want to need, forced to choice, outcome to process, and stress is a difference in perceptions, you will begin to choose different interpretations of what you are perceiving.

While watching the football game, do you have **control** over winning, or do you have the opportunity to enjoy viewing superior athletic skills? But, you have a bet, and your team is losing! What **need** will be fulfilled from successful gambling? Worth! Are there other choices to generate worth if you are losing? Can you keep statistics and feel intelligent when you describe the actions taking place?

Are you **forced** to feel bad because your team is losing, or do you feel bad because you are losing worth? Is expressing anger, no matter how slight, a way you have **chosen** to get worth back? Can you rethink that input changes from moment to moment and this game, like life, is always changing? Is one point in time, the outcome, that important, or is it just another point in the **process** of the day?

Finally, can you rethink that this input is creating a difference between what you need and what you have? The **difference** is why you feel stressed or frustrated, not the game. Can you choose to take control and close the difference by rethinking **control, needs, choices, and process** over what you are taking in? With a change in the interpretation of what you are perceiving, your actions or output choices can be more easily rethought.

When Olive first came into my office, she weighed ninety-two pounds, was about five foot, six inches tall, and looked as though she had just come out of a concentration camp. Olive's physical appearance alone was enough to get a rise out of the most detached observer. Beyond her physical appearance, Olive had little to command attention or to fulfill her needs for belonging and worth.

A traditional approach to Olive's anorexia would probably reinforce positive behavior and punish negative behavior towards food. For example, a traditionalist would praise Olive every time she ate. Praising may work, but would depend on her perceiving praising as satisfying belonging, and her evaluation that eating would not cause a significant loss in other needs. Punishment creates a reduction of behavior. In some hospitals electric shock has been used to punish, but withdrawal, or criticism, is a much more frequent choice. With punishment, Olive would lose belonging, security, faith, and worth. To avoid the loss of these needs, she may choose to eat, or she may not. Change will depend on her internal need state and her interpretation of the best way to meet her needs.

I tried at one time to set up a reward/punishment program to help anorexics. I remember making luncheon appointments at restaurants, hoping to stimulate interest in any type of food. I would order an elaborate meal of enticing, well-prepared foods and try to get them to follow suit. A good idea you might say. Well, not really. Most of the time I would just overeat and gain weight, and my clients would order iced tea with lemon, no sugar.

Olive's parents and friends had already tried that frustrating game of putting food before her, hoping she would eat. Her mother told me about fixing elaborate home-cooked meals and always having freshly baked chocolate chip cookies when she came over. Her father took her out to fine restaurants, also with no success. Her parents were gaining the weight, just as I used to, and getting more frustrated in the process. Olive continued to go without food and lose more weight. Her parents gave her time, attention, took her to doctors, and worried. She got caring and approaching from friends and relatives. Now, why in the world would Olive choose to give up all the control she had over her environment?

While working with Olive, I asked myself, "What does Olive **really want**?" My response was that Olive wanted much of what she was getting—security, worth, and belonging.

What was Olive giving up? In order to fulfill those other needs, she was paying the price of health, fun, freedom, knowledge, and the real security of being able to make positive choices. Her life became more and more limited. Ultimately her physical condition would result in hospitalization unless her **thinking** changed.

Soon I realized how few social skills Olive had. She was very shy and introverted and had no idea how to approach anyone or begin a conversation. She could barely make eye contact. Having so few skills, she perceived herself as an unfriendly person, yet needed pathways to get belonging. The price of the pathway she chose could have been her life!

She used her physical weakness and sickly state as an excuse for not being able to give friendship. In a friendship, it is necessary to demonstrate consideration of and commitment to the friend. With limited approaching skills, few people would choose her as the person through whom they could fulfill their need for belonging.

Olive was supported by her wealthy father and had little need to learn to achieve or develop survival skills. He could easily furnish an apartment for his daughter and pay her bills. Her parents were divorced and involved in beginning lives without her, that is before her anorexia brought them all back together.

The problem wasn't "out there." Nor was it that Olive had a hard time making friends, that she had no work to enrich her, or that she didn't get enough attention from her parents. **The problem was Olive believed she had few skills for satisfying her needs efficiently**. Her thoughts were focused on changing others, not on choices she could make to take responsible control of her life.

One of Olive's big complaints was she just couldn't get her parents to care about her the way she wanted. The only real control Olive had was how she satisfied her need for love by giving it to them. Yet when I suggested that to her, her reaction was, "Why should I show them I care when they don't really care about me?" With that thought in her mind (input), Olive could only take irresponsible actions (output). Until she could rethink to learn other pathways to meet her needs, that thought would persist.

"Would you like to live a long, happy life?" I asked one day. "Is that what you really want?"

Olive answered sadly, "Yes, but I'm sick."

I asked her, "Do you have to be? Could you make the choice to be well?"

Using the Skill Development process, I began to teach Olive the thinking and acting skills to satisfy her needs. We started by looking at the differences between what she wanted and what she had. That motivated her to listen to me discuss what she had complete control over, what she could influence, and what she could neither control nor influence. I asked her to start a list, right there in my office, of what control and influence she had in her life. She was to continue working on the list for the next week.

Once she began to see the difference between control and influence, her thoughts started to change enough for me to teach her about needs. When I presented the Skill Building philosophy, "Everything we think and do is directed toward meeting our internal needs," and described each of the eight needs and the difference between wants and needs, Olive was on her way to rethinking.

Since Olive felt victimized so much of the time, I taught her there is no such thing as being forced to do or feel something. "You made me love you; I didn't want to do it," may be a good song lyric, but in terms of meeting your needs, it is totally inaccurate. Olive would say, "My father made me so angry," or "People aren't friendly," or "I can't help being so thin." **Olive chose angering and anorexia because she believed they were the best ways to meet her needs**.

There's no such animal as "have to," "must," or "should." No one can **make** us think what we think, do what we do, or feel what we feel. No matter how it may look, we **choose** our wants, our perceptions (input), and actions (output). Our feelings, although perhaps not directly chosen, will be based on efficient or inefficient input and output.

Maybe you've found yourself saying goodbye to your spouse in the morning with, "Well, I **have** to go to work now." Perhaps you say, "I **can't** be late for this appointment," or "I **must** have dinner on the table by six." Our language is riddled with terms that imply we are not free to make choices. Actually, all of those statements are inaccurate, since no one is forcing us to go to work, be punctual, or be responsible.

If we alter our language, it might help us remember that our perceptions of what we want and our actions, are choices. For example, instead of making "angry" an adjective, "She made me angry," turn it into a verb. "**I am angering** to meet my need for worth." By making the picture in our head an **active** one, rethinking, "I am depressing," instead of the passive, "You make me depressed," it is easier to perceive we are choosing a feeling or action to best meet our needs. The use of the "ing" form was pioneered by Buckminster Fuller in his book, *I Seem To Be A Verb*. In becoming conscious of how language can inhibit us from choosing efficient pathways, we can rethink what we say to reflect our new perspective. More needs can be met from a position of control than a position of helplessness.

How many of us make choices that in retrospect are foolish and unhealthy? When we are unaware of the purpose behind our reactions, feelings, and thoughts, we end up in a self-destructive cycle. In order to choose wants, perceptions, and actions that are efficient to meet our needs, we can evaluate how our reactions are inefficient. Until we change our perception of our world, we will continue to meet our internal needs through **old reaction habits** which may be injurious.

Have you found yourself reacting in any of the following ways?

ANGERING:	yelling, hitting, threatening, criticizing, punishing, getting even, rejecting, powering, passively-aggressing, swearing.
DEPRESSING:	withdrawing, crying, being alone, self-pitying, complaining.
SOMATIC PAINING:	back/head/stomach/aching, feeling nauseated, having diarrhea, hypertensing, allergically reacting, getting colds, throwing up, refusing to eat, having insomnia, oversleeping.
BURNING OUT:	giving up, malingering, procrastinating, sabotaging, excuse-making.
FEARING:	avoiding, hiding, developing phobias, dropping out.
ACTING INSECURE:	self-doubting, giving control of your life to others, intimidating, controlling others, hesitating, over-spending.
SUBSTANCE ABUSING:	drinking, drugging (legal **or** illegal), overeating, smoking.

BEHAVING SUICIDAL:	threatening to kill yourself, suicidal thinking, hurting yourself.
ACTING CRAZY:	hallucinating, rocking, pacing, silencing, picking fights, making faces.

If you recognize some of these behaviors as your own, it might help to realize these actions are the ways people choose to meet their needs by attempting to control others. All of them usually carry a negative price and must be considered potentially inefficient.

Take **ANGERING**. Angering has many forms, from a direct attack to passive behavior. All anger at traffic, dogs, flat tires, weather, or whatever, is directed to prevent someone or something from controlling you, and to put yourself in the driver's seat. Anger is a direct reaction to meet the need for worth. When you yell and point a finger, you usually are successful at grabbing someone's attention. A person will listen when you steam-roll over him, power over him, or threaten. By choosing to react with angering, you get your need met immediately. You momentarily feel control and self-worth, but the negative price is loss of fulfillment in other areas, and that loss follows quickly. Think about the body language when one person is angering at another. The recipient moves away from the angerer, usually adopting a defensive stance. I can't imagine anyone moving toward someone who is yelling, criticizing, or threatening. Who wants to hug an attacker? So the first need lost through angering is belonging. Even if the angerer gets his subject to do what he wants, how long will they continue? I know I wouldn't do what someone "bossed" me into doing for long. I might even sabotage the outcome if I were coerced into doing something after I had been angered at. Also, I wouldn't continue to feel the same way about the person who was doing the angering. I might mistrust him in the future, and my behavior around him would no longer be free and humorous. Now the angering person has lost two more needs—freedom and fun.

The angering person also compromises his health through such reactions. Many somatic changes occur when people try to control others and their environment through angering. Often angering results in rising blood pressure, intestinal disorders, allergic reactions, and perhaps heart attacks. Studies indicate that there might be a link between some forms of cancer and angering.

When anger is held in, it becomes passive-aggressive behavior. Passive-aggressing is an attempt to control others. Suppose your little Erick hates peas. He can get "even" with you for putting the nasty green things on his plate by pushing them around, dropping them on the floor, mashing them up, or gagging on them. Here you are, a full grown adult seated across from a child less than three feet tall. Who is in control of this dinner table? Who has the power? You can choose to react to the situation by turning red in the face, by snapping at him, "Don't you know that peas are good for you, and I only want you to grow up healthy?" You could also pull him out of his chair and send him to his room. Or, you can choose to meet your need for belonging at the dinner table by talking to Erick. If you and Erick can find a green vegetable he likes, no one will have to control how any one else lives. By changing perceptions, you can choose a different action to efficiently meet your needs.

Picture yourself on a street corner waiting for the red light to turn green. It's a busy intersection, and cars are whizzing past you. Suddenly, you are pushed from behind, and you lurch into the street. What are you feeling? Are you angry, do you think, "Who the hell did that? Am I going to give that so-and-so a piece of my mind!"? After all, your health was endangered and your self-worth violated. You turn around, ready to verbally blast someone. But then you see a young girl standing with a white cane and dark glasses, one hand frantically pushing out to feel if anything is in front of her. What do you feel at that moment? Has something happened to your anger? Here is a small girl with a look of fear on her face, sightlessly trying to make her way across a busy street. She had mistakenly pushed a pedestrian into the traffic. I suspect your angering changed or that it dissipated. When your perception of the situation changed, you no longer chose to gain self-worth through angering. Your perceptions enabled you to rethink, and angering was bypassed for compassion.

A change in perceptions can also rid one of the behavioral habit of **DEPRESSING**. Depressing, without a significant biochemical precedent, is another of those chosen behaviors that usually costs more than it's worth. Like angering, depressing works to get attention. A person who is withdrawing from a friend or spouse will usually succeed in having that person approach to ask, "What's wrong? What can I do to help?" They might actually try to make some fun in an attempt to get him to laugh or smile and feel better. The immediate reward of depressing is belonging.

Depressing is certainly more efficient than angering because people aren't immediately repelled by it. However, if it becomes chronic, people eventually stay away. Who wants to be around someone who's walking on his chin or who always has a dark cloud around his head? The negative price far outweighs the positive, since the end result of depressing is a loss of worth, security, fun, and eventually, belonging. Since depressing people are often sedentary, it isn't too good for health either. Depressing people don't usually say, "Well, I think I'll put aside my depressing, so I can go out and ride a bike."

Depressing has been a choice in our culture for a very long time, and it will continue to be a choice until people discover alternative perceptions and actions to meet their needs, especially the need for belonging. I could choose depressing whenever I want to control Suzy. Like many husbands, I could hang my head, withdraw, complain, rather than participate in a conversation with her. She might suggest I travel too much. She might tell me how worried she is that I work too hard. Would I get her to give me attention and concern by complaining, "Oh, I have so much on my mind right now—there's a seminar today, tonight I have to be in Carmel, and I don't know if I can make it on time. I'm really pressured, and I want to be left alone."? Yes, I would get her attention. But I would meet more of my needs by taking fifteen minutes and spending quality time with her to demonstrate my concern. I would be more in-control of my life if I made a plan for an evening out that would benefit the two of us. It would meet my needs efficiently to rethink and take action to feel worth, security, health, and belonging. It would also give me freedom from the limitations that depressing imposes.

SOMATIC PAINING should be reason enough for changing your behavior. Some loss of need fulfillment is inevitable when you are physically hurting. There was a time when I worked with two clients of almost the same age. One was active and robust; the other was sickly and paining. The contrast was remarkable. Each came to me with feelings of loneliness. Both had recently lost their spouses, and I thought needed to start evaluating the perceptions of their world, then rethink to develop more control and put more belonging into their lives. They both felt lonely, but the loneliness came out for the paining client as a series of illnesses, aches, and outbursts of self-pity. She complained of varicose veins, stiff joints, backaches, dental problems, and skin rashes. There were no major organic problems, but she had a collection of nagging ailments that "made" her too tired to do much of anything. Her children lived close by, yet she rarely saw them and bitterly resented the way they had "turned their backs now that she was old and sick." She said she had given her whole life for them, and now that she needed them to take care of her, everyone was too busy with their own lives. She spent the day in her housecoat, shuffling around an empty house, now and then watching soap operas. Why bother getting dressed when it hurt her joints so much? Besides, who was there to get dressed for? Her weight had jumped nearly twenty pounds in the seven months since her husband had died.

The active client, on the other hand, was a positive woman who was very descriptive in talking about the six grandchildren she "loved to death." In addition to the time she spent nurturing her family, this woman took great pride in her Saturday night bowling league and her talent for needlepoint, which she hoped she might turn into a money-making hobby.

Since her husband died, she didn't get out as much as she would have liked, but she managed to work out on an exercise bike every morning to stay in shape. Originally she came to my office complaining of too much time on her hands, especially at night when she was home alone. This woman got most of her needs met so efficiently during the day, it was a piece of cake to teach her thinking and acting skills.

The client who tried to meet her needs by negative actions had to learn that paining, complaining, and being sickly were causing her to pay a tremendous price for what little need fulfillment she was producing. If her perceptions continued in this mode, there was a very strong possibility that her body would actually break down.

A classic example of somatic paining is choosing anorexia or bulimia. Remember Olive, the girl who tried to control her family and environment by refusing to eat? Anorexia and bulimia are ways of meeting needs that can cost the ultimate, your life. Karen Carpenter, a successful singer with many loyal fans, died as a result of bulimia. It was a terrible waste.

Another terrible waste of time and talent is to choose **BURNING OUT** as a source of need fulfillment. Many people believe that "burning out" must be an inevitable consequence of working in today's world. If the pressure of living in a fast-paced world seems overwhelming, if we feel out-of-control regarding demands or hassles at work or home, it makes sense to choose burning out as a way to feel better.

Burning out means that we think, "I give up." It happens when we believe our needs are fulfilled by people or things "out there." If only your boss and co-workers would behave more appropriately, if only so much wasn't expected of you, if only your workload were lighter, if only the system were to change, if only your kids or spouse were more cooperative, then you'd feel more in-control and have more security and worth. Right? Could be. The problem is, you can't control "out there" to change in a positive direction to get enough of what you need. Burning out is a good excuse to cover up mistakes or inefficiencies. Suppose your manager and co-workers notice you're less productive; you make mistakes; you forget important meetings. They suspect you're even sabotaging some projects. You begin to complain and procrastinate, coming in later and later after lunch. So your manager calls you into his office. His manner is concerned, sympathetic. "Paul, is there anything wrong?" he asks kindly.

"I feel burned out," you tell him very seriously, "don't seem to be able to keep up anymore." Your boss, usually very distant and professional, starts acting differently. He listens, asks questions, even seems to agree with your laments. Aha! Now you've gained control. But have you?

Look at the prices paid for being in a weak position at work. Even though you may have gained a temporary reprieve, there is no job that is going to accept inefficiency, lack of productivity, procrastination, tardiness, or hangers-on for very long. You may learn an extensive repertoire of excuse-making behavior, but you will also jeopardize your livelihood. Although burning out may temporarily reduce the pressure of the job and even put off getting fired, it certainly isn't a long-term solution. The loss from burning out is the risk of giving up real self-worth, security, additional knowledge, fun, freedom, and health. You can see how inefficient burning out can be compared to choosing to rethink what you really have control of at work and home, meeting all of your needs.

FEARING may be even less efficient than burning out as a pathway to meet our needs. Have you ever heard a story of someone who hid in some hovel most of his life and was found dead, lying on a mattress stuffed with hundred dollar bills? Or did you know that the famous writer of science fiction, Ray Bradbury, has such a phobia of machines that he never learned to drive and has never flown in a plane? How about an entire generation that was so afraid of the challenges of society that it dropped out for a decade? It may not look like fearing of this sort meets many of our needs, but it does. It doesn't meet them efficiently, but fearing can get us belonging, the feeling of security, worth, and sometimes fun. The person who never steps out of the house has to recruit a lot of people to wait on her just to survive. The fear may be so severe that it imprisons her, yet she can still pick up the phone and feel belonging and worth when she gets people to cater to her needs. Does she pay any negative prices for her phobia?

Ray Bradbury gets a lot of mileage out of his phobias. When he addresses his audiences, his fear of flying is a great conversation piece and an ironic contrast to his writing. Imagine the man who wrote *The Martian Chronicles,* and who christened the first space shuttle, being terrified of airplanes. How unique it makes him never to have driven a car! Bradbury may pay the price of freedom (going distances takes him ten times as long, and he must have people chauffeur him everywhere), of some worth, some security, some knowledge, but he sure knows how to get belonging and love by captivating audiences. I prefer having as many alternatives and choices as possible. Fearing is just too high a price to pay in order to have belonging.

I bet you can recall coming to aid a friend who was **ACTING INSECURE**. Someone says to you, "I can't do it. I know I can't do it," and bursts into tears.

You rush over and reassure them, "Sure you can. I know you can do it! I have faith in you. All you have to do is try, and I know you'll do it!"

The person keeps crying, insisting, "No, I can't."

"Yes you can," you repeat. And the "No-I-can't," "Yes-you-can," cheerleading routine goes on for what seems like forever. Does this sound familiar? Who is in-control in this situation? What is the purpose of acting insecure? Mr. or Ms. Insecure is getting belonging and faith through your caring. You're probably getting tired. If such behavior goes on too long, you'll get frustrated and leave.

Although each of us has moments of feeling insecure, and benefit from support by friends, it's a losing choice if acting insecure is the only way to get love. It calls for continually demeaning one's self, "Poor me, I don't know how to do anything," an attitude that will destroy self-worth or security. Again, a person who chooses acting insecure is not going to have people around for long. It's just too unpleasant to be around someone who knocks himself all the time. It can become another self-fulfilling prophecy, so that everyone, including you, will believe you're not worth much after all. It's difficult to build a successful career by acting insecure. In fact, it will be nearly impossible to succeed in anything with such an inefficient choice. Acting insecure as a long-term pathway to meet your needs will probably result in losing everything.

SUBSTANCE-ABUSING is another no-win choice. When I started undergraduate work at Loyola University, I fortuitously applied for a job in the television industry which turned out to be fun, exciting, and an invigorating learning experience. My job title was "language coordinator." Impressive, huh? I'll tell you a secret—a language coordinator prints and holds cue cards! I worked on variety shows and met most of the big-name stars in the late Fifties and early Sixties. One was Dean Martin, who truly earned his reputation. The man was funny, easy-going, certainly had charisma—and always a glass in his hand. I recall how he'd say, "I feel sorry for people who don't drink, because when they get up in the morning, that's as as good as they're going to feel all day!

Drinking or drugging makes people feel "good," or they wouldn't do it. You don't see people drinking Drano to have a good time. The use of too much alcohol or drugs works on the central nervous system, inhibiting the mind from clearly perceiving differences. Under the influence of such substances, your mind can no longer discriminate between what you need and what you perceive in the environment. You recall that stress is the difference between what you need and what you have. If the substances blur or erase that perceptual difference, then the abuser will feel less stress.

The process of reducing our perceptual differences makes us feel good. Substances are quick reducers of feelings of inadequacy, insecurity, loneliness, tension, helplessness, and general paining. Whatever the substance happens to be, including food in overeating, the price is always the same—the person's health and well-being suffers. If the substance-abusing goes on too long, work and family are disrupted, costing the abuser loss of belonging, worth, and security. Permanent injury or death can occur from prolonged substance-abuse. Such a choice just doesn't efficiently meet our needs.

Learning to rethink might not be as instant a cure for the stresses of daily living, but it allows us to develop a more effective strategy to meet our needs forever. It's fun to sink our teeth into some luscious chocolates, but it's no fun to try to find a suit to fit a three hundred and fifty pound body. Substance-abusing is a one-way street to destruction, no matter how good it may feel for a moment.

I have encountered three different types of people who were **BEHAVING SUICIDAL** to meet their needs. The first I call "to be," the second "to be or not to be," and the third, "not to be." The "to be" is a person who is in such great pain he sees no alternatives for feeling better. This person doesn't talk to others about his suicidal plans. He will actually jump off a twenty-story building or stick a gun in his mouth and pull the trigger. For a "to be," the decision to end his life actually gives him relief. Because he can't think of alternatives to feel better, the decision will motivate him to successfully kill himself. This may seem like a drastic way to control others' behavior, yet the "to be" type sometimes uses his self-murder to make someone feel guilty, or to punish others. It's even possible that the "to be" will kill himself right in front of the person he wants to control, to horrify, or hurt. Unfortunately, he will never really know if he has "gotten even." By the way, the awful thing about "getting even" is that you're just even, not ahead! The "to be" may believe that his pain will be reduced by committing suicide, but the reality is that he prevented himself from discovering the true pleasure of finding positive choices to meet the rest of his needs.

The "to be or not to be" are also in great pain, but they are ambivalent about whether or not they want to kill themselves. Unlike the first type, they have not yet decided that there is no other way to feel better. They may begin an attempt, then change their minds. "To be or not to be" are not sure death is the final solution, and so they arrange rescue. This type feels his self-worth is enhanced by having people "save" him at the eleventh hour—if he gets saved. I believe Marilyn Monroe was a "to be or not to be" who didn't get help in time. There are thousands who change their minds too late.

The "not to be" do not intend to kill themselves. Talking suicide is a way to have people care for them, a way to shock or startle, and a way to gain attention and importance. The "not to be" make overt threats or subtle hints. They talk about wills, objects they want their friends to have when they die, funeral plans, or other morbid thoughts. Then, if they are about to slit a wrist or take a pill, they call friends or professionals, leaving many messages. By the time they act, the "not to be" is sure someone is on the other side of the bathroom door. Unfortunately, some also succeed in killing themselves, simply because the person on the other side can't break down the door fast enough to stop the bleeding, or they find their friend too late.

Behaving suicidally is a no-win proposition, since success means death. A risky business, even for the "not to be." A person who does so is screaming out that they have few perceptions and acting skills to meet their needs.

ACTING CRAZY may not seem like efficient behavior, but I assure you that it is a powerful way to control others. Imagine waiting at a bus stop and seeing someone pacing or speaking out loud to himself. Don't you find yourself curious, choosing to stare a little? A woman walks around my neighborhood wearing a tin foil hat and lives out of a shopping cart. She argues with parked cars or bushes. Sometimes she even steps into the street to chase a car. Confess, are you intrigued by this woman's bizarre actions? I wonder if at some time in your life acting crazy worked to get one or more of your needs met. Perhaps you didn't go so far as to chase cars, but you might have acted crazy to get someone to listen to you, or maybe you behaved slightly crazy to generate fun in a boring situation. Many people choose appearing crazy to get out of a painful situation, rather than finding more efficient tools for security and worth. Acting crazy is such a successful pathway to meet our needs by controlling what others think, do, and feel, we may get more than we bargain for. In the movie *One Flew Over the Cuckoo's Nest,* you'll remember how good Jack Nicholson was at acting crazy—so good that they locked him up and threw away the key. The main characters in that movie were able to avoid responsibility, but one of them nearly lost his life, and the other lost his ability to think. Acting crazy is too costly a way to meet the needs of belonging, worth, and fun. It means gambling big with your freedom, security, and health.

In case you wonder if acting crazy is a choice, I'll share an experience I had while working at Camarillo State Hospital. I observed many severely disturbed patients, and I noticed that none of them, no matter how disturbed they might be, acted crazy **all** the time. Even the most erratic person had moments of acting "normal." In retrospect, I realize that even seriously disturbed people don't act crazy all the time because their needs can be met in other ways. Sometimes they perceive that "normal" pathways may not give them what they want, so they choose crazy alternatives that with time become habits for an unfulfilled lifestyle.

When the pathways to meet your needs are reactions you have programmed into your brain (habits), you choose the kinds of out-of-control behavior I have described in this chapter. The consequence will be a loss of personal power. Skill Builders learn to make efficient choices to meet their needs. Instead of **must**, a Skill Builder thinks I **choose**. Instead of **should**, a Skill Builder thinks I **prefer**. Below are some other words which promote change from a forced or victim perception, to a responsible, in-control perception.

I choose	I will	I do
I decide	I promote	I start
I want	I seek	I stop
I can	I practice	I am

To rethink your choices, you can first decide that what you are now thinking and doing is not bringing you enough happiness. You can decide to be more than just comfortable. If you make the **value judgment** that you don't want to be a WhMPA, settling for inefficient choices like Angering, Depressing, Somatic Paining, Burning Out, Fearing, Acting Insecure, Substance-Abusing, Behaving Suicidal, and Acting Crazy, then you can begin to develop rethinking skills. You can start right now. Before you put this book down, before you choose any other action, you can start making choices about the life you want, or you can wait . . .

CHAPTER FIVE

Outcome to Process Person

> "After I_____ , then I'll have it made."
>
> WhMPA

WhMPA Multiple Choice Fill In (for the above sentence).

1. Get a driver's license
2. Get into college
3. Reach twenty-one
4. Get out of school
5. Get a job
6. Leave home
7. Get married
8. Get divorced
9. Have a family
10. Become successful
11. Win the lottery
12. Get the kids to leave
13. Retire
14. Get to heaven

> "Happiness is not a state to arrive at, but a manner of traveling."
>
> Margaret Lee Runbeck

Tucked away in our subconscious is an idyllic vision. We see ourselves on a long trip that spans the continent. We are traveling by train. Out the windows we drink in the passing scene of cars on nearby highways, of children waving at a crossing, of cattle grazing on a distant hillside, of smoke pouring from a power plant, of row upon row of corn and wheat, of flatlands and valleys, of mountains and rolling hillsides, of city skylines and village halls.

But uppermost in our minds is the final destination. On a certain day at a certain hour we will pull into the station. Bands will be playing and flags waving. Once we get there so many wonderful dreams will come true and the pieces of our lives will fit together like a completed jigsaw puzzle. How restlessly we pace the aisles, damning the minutes for loitering - waiting, waiting, waiting for the station.

"When we reach the station, that will be it!" we cry. "When I'm 18." "When I buy a new 450 SL Mercedes Benz!" "When I put the last kid through college." "When I have paid off the mortgage!" "When I get a promotion." "When I reach the age of retirement, I shall live happily ever after!"

Sooner or later we must realize there is no station, no one place to arrive at once and for all. The true joy of life is the trip. The station is only a dream. It constantly outdistances us.

"Relish the moment" is a good motto, especially when coupled with Psalm 118:24: "This is the day which the Lord hath made; we will rejoice and be glad in it." It isn't the burdens of today that drive men mad. It is the regrets over yesterday and the fear of tomorrow. Regret and fear are twin thieves who rob us of today.

So, stop pacing the aisles and counting the miles. Instead, climb more mountains, eat more ice cream, go barefoot more often, swim more rivers, watch more sunsets, laugh more, cry less. Life must be lived as we go along. The station will come soon enough.

The Station, by
Robert J. Hastings

"The true joy of life is the trip," Robert Hastings wrote in his essay. We don't have to wait for a knight on a white horse to sweep us away or a financial windfall before we can be happy. **Today** is the most important day of our life. To make today the happiest day of our life, we can adopt the strategy of meeting our needs now. That strategy is the process of Skill Building.

Sometimes it seems the whole world is designed toward the future instead of focusing on living today. Do you recall being fifteen and a half, and waiting, waiting, waiting for your sixteenth birthday to finally get that prized possession—real freedom—the driver's license? And how many people count the days until they're twenty-one, so they can walk into a bar and challenge the bartender to ask for an I.D.? Now they can drink and drive! How often have you heard someone say, "I'm almost twenty-five, it's time to think about getting married."? Surely you know parents who can't wait until their teenagers are in college, so they can finally have some peace and quiet. I'm confident you've heard someone say how anxious he was for retirement to do all those things he's been putting off for years. It seems everyone has these check points they're waiting for because life is supposed to be better once some event occurs.

Even if it's just watching the clock at work, counting the minutes until quitting time, you're giving up the enjoyment that takes place between the nine o'clock drag and the five o'clock dash. If you are wrapped up in a hot date for Saturday night and spend all week only anticipating Saturday, what happens to Monday through Friday?

There's nothing wrong in looking toward the future, in planning goals and activities for yourself. But if the future dominates your thinking, if you believe happiness is only in the future, you are stuck waiting for a future that may never come, and you ignore good process in the present.

If you think happiness is tomorrow or next weekend, or an upcoming event, I have two words for you:

DON'T WAIT!

When you are in the process of meeting all your needs in every situation, you are making every minute count. You don't need to find joy in some projected future excitement, nor will you depend on others to make your life work.

WhMPAs settle for a reduced return on their life invest-ment because they choose to wait. Skill Builders don't settle because they're working to meet all their needs efficiently in any situation or environment.

An example of the "waiting-to-feel-good syndrome" is Bob. As an engineer for a large aircraft corporation, Bob worked hard all his life, sacrificing today to feel better tomor-row. He looked forward to the time when his children were gone, the mortgage on his house was paid, and he was reaping the benefits of his company's pension plan—the "golden years" WhMPAs dream about.

Bob was in the early months of retirement when I first met him. He appeared to be in good health. His blue eyes sparkled as he told me about his achievements and his grandchildren. However, the sparkle left as he talked about retirement. I asked him to tell me more about his life. What had he done for fun and excitement? Bob thought a moment, brushed back his thinning hair, sighed and said, "You know, all I did was work. Fun? Freedom? Excitement? That's what you work for all your life. You get most of that after you've retired, or at least that's what I always believed."

I continued questioning, "Well, can you think of important times that really stand out in your memory?"

Bob thought again. "The day I was married—that was a big day. The birth of my first child—I got that son I wanted so badly!" He added. "Of course, the time I bought my first house was really a big deal, too." He smiled at this memory, "My wife would kill me if I didn't mention our twenty-fifth wedding anniversary. But the real prize was that retirement dinner! I can still see myself listening to the boss make one of those speeches which makes you emotional and turn red be-cause it's about you. Well, I was caught up with that, but at the same time I was thinking, 'Finally you've got it made, Bob—freedom! The kids are gone; the house is paid off; pension's going to be coming in; you've really got it made old boy.' But you know, the strange thing is, I feel like I'm at the last chap-ter of my life, the so-called big payoff, and it's like I haven't really lived at all. I should be enjoying life. Hell, that's what I worked for all my life, but it isn't going that way. Everything's a big blur. I'm starting to get pains in my leg, headaches, sometimes I'm even bored."

It was obvious that Bob's "golden years" were beginning to tarnish. I moved on to ask feeling questions. "When were you happy? Were you ever happy at work?"

He stared at me, "Happy at work? Work is what you do to make money. That's it. You work hard all your life, then retire and have time to relax—no hassles! You reap the rewards of all that work."

I continued questioning. "Were there times, Bob, when you'd watch the clock at work, waiting for closing?"

Bob chuckled, "Doesn't everyone? Yeah, I watched that clock, especially when the boss was angry, and always, always on Fridays."

"Always on Fridays?"

"Sure, you know, for the weekend. TGIF, freedom for two whole days!"

"Does freedom come from 'out there' or from our perceptions?" I asked. Bob, like many clients I've encountered, was puzzled by this question. I continued, "Do you play any sports?" He told me he had played golf with the same foursome for many years. I asked him to tell me the best thing about playing golf. He said he loved to beat the foursome out of the money they bet, and he always enjoyed improving his score. In all phases of Bob's life, he was into "outcomes." I asked how long it took for him to play golf, and he estimated about five and a half hours.

"If you win, you really feel great, right?"

Bob's eyes regained their twinkle, "You'd better believe it!"

I asked him how long that good feeling lasted, and he replied, "About five minutes."

"So you spend five and a half hours, and only if you win, you feel good for five minutes. Does that seem like an efficient way to get enjoyment in your life?"

Bob's eyes lost their twinkle again, "Sounds kind of dumb, doesn't it? Especially since I get so upset with my poor shots. I also seem to have problems with my back from my drives. Just part of the aging process, I guess."

At this point I knew it was time to ask him a very important value judgment question, so that he could begin to evaluate his behavior. "Bob, has waiting for the future given you **enough** happiness?"

He thought for a few moments, then said, "No."

"What do you **really want,** Bob?"

"Something I've never really had in my life—to relax and feel good about living my life without worrying about tomorrow."

Like many people, Bob had put off feeling good and enjoying living through meeting his needs. His expectation of those "golden years" didn't equal the reality of living them. All his life he had worked for outcome, not **process.**

Before I developed the Skill Building strategy, I would have immediately signed Bob up for lots of "doing" plans: join a Senior Citizens group take out a "Y" membership and participate in some classes, volunteer time with deprived children, do some traveling. Now, there is nothing wrong with any of those plans if the individual chooses to do them. WhMPAs, however, looking to "out there" to fulfill their needs, frequently try these things, get disappointed, and quit.

Once a person begins to recognize the frustration in waiting for outcomes, I am able to introduce the fourth area of rethinking—working to be in process. Remember, change begins when you **evaluate your world and perceive a difference between what you need and how things are. With a perceptual difference you can then begin to rethink what you could think and do differently to feel better.**

Can you see some of yourself in Bob? Are you waiting too much for the future to bring you the happiness you deserve? If waiting does not bring you enough fulfillment, I suggest you begin to think of life as a process where you behave differently in each of your environments. For example, your home, car, job, or recreational facility are opportunities to take control and rethink what you can do to meet your needs.

Ask yourself each morning as you wake up, "What will I choose today to meet as many of my eight internal needs as possible? Evaluating your present behavior is very helpful to begin your rethinking process to make a plan. Are you rolling out of bed grumbling about the day? Do you take a quick, routine shower, and while shaving or making up, feel older and less attractive? Do you gulp down a cup of coffee and rush out the door wondering why you are stuck in this rat race?

Would you rather relax and read the paper? Do you wish it were Sunday? No wonder work-day mornings are painful! With a painful evaluation of your actions, you are ready to rethink how to get more need fulfillment in the first hour of your day.

Must you wait for Sunday mornings to feel better? Could you wake up to music from a clock radio and, while still lying in bed, collect your thoughts and begin to make positive plans about what you are going to do that day to meet all of your needs? This may sound silly, especially if you have no time, or some other **excuse** as to why you can't start to rethink. Silly as it may sound, it's a choice you can make.

While showering, can you whistle or sing and enjoy the warm water massaging your body? (**Fun**) Could you look for your positive physical qualities in the mirror when you shave or put on your make-up? (**Faith**) In the background, could a radio or television bring you new information for the day as you blow dry your hair? (**Knowledge**) Could you take vitamins and drink fresh juice? (**Health**) Could you smile and say, "Good morning," to the first person you see? (**Belonging**) Might you have a list of new achievements and routine chores with you as you leave your home? (**Worth and Security**) These are choices about which you first **rethink** and then, maybe, on which you act. (**Freedom**)

When you reach your car or bus for your thirty minute ride to work, could you think of your vehicle as a classroom for **Security, Faith, Worth, Freedom, Belonging, Fun, Knowledge,** and **Health**? Could you listen to audio tapes that give information about more efficiently meeting your needs? Cassette tapes are available in many categories: motivational, health, relationships, comedy, trivia, specific subjects such as business and foreign languages—yes, even Skill Building! There is a service which reports in-depth interviews and information in the news for the past week. Of course, you may not have a tape machine in your car, or perhaps you ride a bus or subway. You, I guess, will have to **wait** for your need fulfillment if you think WhMPA thoughts. Skill Builders never wait for need fulfillment. If they don't have a tape recorder or a radio available, they can sing their own songs, practice a speech, or write out an achievement plan. If a Skill Builder is a strap hanger, he can engage a fellow passenger in conversation. While sitting, he can read the paper, a book, notes, or even try imagining the occupations or marital status of the other passengers. Going to work is need fulfilling if you think process.

At work, do you get need fulfillment each day? If not, start the process **right now** by rethinking what you are going to do to meet each one of your eight needs tomorrow at work. Check yourself out on the list below:

NEED	WHAT YOU CAN DO AT WORK
SECURITY:	building skills that you control _____
	_____
FAITH:	seeing the positive _____
	_____
WORTH:	taking a risk to achieve beyond _____ where you are
	_____
FREEDOM:	seeing respon- sible choices _____
	_____
BELONGING:	approaching others first _____
	_____
FUN:	creating laughter _____
	_____
KNOWLEDGE:	asking questions _____
	_____

HEALTH: walking, not just
            sitting   _____

            _____

When you meet your needs in every environment, you don't wait for tomorrow because you're thinking and feeling good today. It's like a kid on summer vacation at the beach— you hope the day will never end. If you evaluate your world and then rethink new choices, work could feel like a day at the beach. Work, a place where you spend five-sevenths of each week until you retire, could be as fulfilling as being on vacation. Adopting this philosophy can change your whole way of life.

What makes a vacation, whether it's just a weekend or a a month in Europe, so good, so desirable? Have all of them been positive, or have you had times you would love to forget? I have—several in fact, when my vacation goals were very different from what I actually experienced. In other words, I didn't achieve enough need fulfillment. I wasn't in-control. I was passively awaiting fulfillment, not actively choosing to be fulfilled by what I could do.

Can you just sit on a lovely beach for seven days and do nothing but rest, watch the surf, and eat three gourmet meals a day? Some may think so, and for a few days it might be very enjoyable, but most people would soon get bored. A great vacation is need fulfilling. One can laugh (**Fun**), be with people and feel close to them (**Belonging**), see the beauty of nature or what others have created (**Faith**), achieve something, even if it's just catching up on one's reading (**Worth**), exercise (**Health**), enhance old, or learn new skills (**Security**), gather information (**Knowledge**), and do whatever one wants for the day (**Freedom**). I am not pushing any place or any style of vacation. It's your vacation, and you will choose your pathways. But for a fantastic vacation, create a plan to meet as many of your needs as possible. The process of meeting each of your needs in all your different environments takes you out of waiting. The difference in your life is phenomenal. When I was a child, I had a special aunt who was great fun because of her desire to make each moment of the day an adventure. I remember how I would get embarrassed when she spontaneously spoke to strangers or laughed out loud in public places. She taught me we can wait for excitement and joy to happen, or we can make them happen. When I choose to act spontaneously, I always experience need fulfillment.

I'll never forget a plane trip last year from Los Angeles to Chicago where I avoided being self-critical and acted very spontaneously, to my everlasting delight. About twenty minutes out of Los Angeles the pilot announced over the intercom that on the left side of the plane we could see the city of Palm Springs, California. In a little while we heard about the California desert on our right and then the city of Las Vegas. At that point I knew the Grand Canyon was next. I waited in my seat until we were close to the canyon, and then with a smile and a racing heart, I got up, matter-of-factly walked over to the flight attendant's intercom, turned it on and announced to the passengers, "Ladies and gentlemen, those of you on the right side of the aircraft, if you look down you will see the Grand Canyon. Those of you on the left side of the plane, if you will look to your right, you will see your fellow passengers looking—at the Grand Canyon!" I then put the intercom down and calmly walked back to my seat amidst great laughter and applause.

What was behind this somewhat unusual behavior? Had I gone completely mad or maybe truly sane? What I was really choosing to do was allow my present creative perceptions to become immediate actions. I was not concerned with what others might think or of my own self-criticism. Because I was not concerned with outcomes, I enjoyed a very spontaneous and free moment to be me.

We can choose to take control of our thoughts and actions, to make plans for each day and, in the same day, act spontaneously to meet our needs. Making the change to a process person requires some risk, but "the true joy of life is the trip."

CHAPTER SIX

Making Stress A Great Opportunity

"Anything that can go wrong, will go wrong."

Murphy's Law—WhMPA Thought

"The discovery of the nuclear chain reaction need not bring about the destruction of mankind any more than did the discovery of matches."

Albert Einstein

Stress, dreaded enemy of WhMPAs, is with us everyday regardless of who we are or what we do. People have made careers from teaching others how to reduce or cope with inevitable stress—the difference between what they need and what they perceive they have. A major difference between Where Most People Are and Skill Builders is WhMPAs do everything in their power to avoid stress, while Skill Builders deal with stress by **accepting** it as a fact of life, and use it to grow. Sometimes they even choose to create stress because they are rethinking that stress is their friend, an opportunity to help them change and achieve. Stress doesn't teach specific ways to change. It is simply a sign that life is different from a need or goal we have. WhMPAs perceive stress as a "problem" since it reduces their comfort level. Skill Builders perceive stress as the indicator to develop a strategy to become risk-takers and change.

I'll give you a concrete example of two ways to deal with stress. Suppose you drive onto the highway. You are due to meet a business associate in twenty minutes. Your punctuality is part of acting responsibly and presenting a good impression. You think that if you can close this deal there will definitely be a bonus, and you can take your wife to Hawaii for a week's vacation. You're excited and secure with yourself and your presentation. "What a beautiful day!" you say.

Then something happens to upset the balance. All of a sudden, red taillights flash ahead. You crawl to a stop, straining to see what has gone wrong. There is no turn-off for at least another mile, and all you can see ahead of you are lines of parked cars. Five minutes go by, and you have progressed only one car length.

Another five minutes go by. All that extra time you allotted to get to the appointment is gone. The beautiful, sunny day becomes hotter and hotter. The clear air is filled with gas fumes, and you feel increasingly uncomfortable. You start tapping on the steering wheel with impatience, becoming nervous and anxious. It looks as though you have a big problem.

What **really** is the problem? There is a difference between the perception of the world as you have created it in your mind and what you perceive to be happening. Instead of arriving at the appointment on time, cool, clear-headed, and well-prepared for your presentation, you are stuck on the highway, experiencing stress.

If you aren't used to evaluating and rethinking, you could find yourself **reacting** instead of acting. Your reactions might include fighting with the other drivers by honking your horn, swearing out the window, hitting the steering wheel, and making yourself a worried, frantic mess. You can choose to reduce the pain of stress by angering, worrying, or depressing. If you perceive stress as it is—a difference between what you need and what you have—you can take action to meet your needs efficiently. If your needs can only be met by making that appointment, then you might consider pulling your car over to the shoulder, if you can get over, and abandoning it so you can run the mile to the nearest exit and try to grab a cab. It would probably be more efficient to meet your needs through less drastic actions. If you are able to rethink, to determine what you **really** need, you will take the most effective action rather than merely **reacting** to the situation.

As I stated in Chapter Three, we may not always get what we want, but we can always satisfy what we **need** if we can rethink. You want to make that appointment on time, but circumstances have made it impossible. Even if you abandon your car, you won't make it in ten minutes. So you have the **opportunity** to figure out how you can get some fulfillment of self-worth, security, freedom, or some other need right there in the middle of a traffic jam. The stress of the situation has alerted you to come up with alternative actions. When you realize you can take advantage of the time to listen to a tape you've been putting off, you will start to control how you feel. You can't make the traffic move, but you can learn something new, listen to music you enjoy, mentally work through some plan for the afternoon or evening, or even reorganize your presentation for when you finally do arrive at your destination. All of these actions will help you gain back the sense of security you had before the incident. You will begin to feel faith in yourself again, and your sense of worth will be enhanced by recognizing you are in an achieving process, not merely suffering the outcome. **Instead of allowing stress to unbalance you, you have turned the situation around so**

that evaluating your world and rethinking your choices has resulted in meeting your needs in spite of an annoying situation. You have turned a problem into an opportunity for developing skills and satisfying your needs.

Since our problems vary in degree, the difference between what we need and what we perceive we have may be small or large. When the difference is small, such as losing a shirt button or getting a telephone busy signal, the frustration is slight.

Imagine the difference between what you need and what you have is great. Suppose you invest a large amount of money in stocks that go down the next day, or your girlfriend decides to marry another man, or your doctor tells you that you have a serious illness. Would you experience feelings of overwhelming stress or frustration? Of course!

The common way to resolve frustrations of any magnitude is by problem-solving. This can only be an efficient choice part of the time. Most people adopt a lifestyle of attacking problems rather than creating new skills. The reason such a lifestyle doesn't work effectively is that problem-solving is usually directed "out there." By building skills, we focus on **ourselves** and what we do in the here and now. It is an uncommon strategy for living, but it can be learned. **Instead of focusing on changing a person, place, or thing, we can choose to evaluate and rethink our whole selves, rather than one special "problem"**. Problem-solving is an indirect, usually out-of-control way to satisfy our needs. Skill Building is a direct, in-control way to create pathways to meet all our needs all the time.

Remember the notion of people being vehicles who move on eight wheels called needs? What holds the wheels together are the spokes called wants, or pathways to meet those needs. The pathways, as you recall, can be both efficient and inefficient. So we have the vehicle and the wheels, but what makes us run? What is the fuel that turns the wheels?

Human beings are the most successful species on the planet because they can adapt to any situation. People do not have natural equipment to defend themselves as most animals do, yet we don't merely survive, we thrive. What do we have that allows us to live equally well in frozen arctics and arid wastelands? What is the fuel that makes Sammy run whether he lives in Alaska or the Sahara? It isn't merely adaptation. People don't merely adapt to their environments; they keep enhancing and improving them. It isn't merely survival. Eskimos and Bedouins don't just survive; they have elaborate cultures which they have created.

I believe human beings use motivation as fuel, and the basis for motivation is the universal desire to be happy. **We are happy when our needs are met or when we are in the process of meeting them**.

There will be few hours in our lifetime when our needs will be completely fulfilled. Therefore, it is critical to our happiness to think of stress as our friend and as a signal that change, growth, creativity, and adaptation are necessary. Imagine you are now a new species called "Homo Sapiens" just at the beginning of civilization, watching some Neanderthal lugging a stone from a quarry to his cave. You're sitting there exhausted from lugging your own stone up the hill to the hut you built. Both of you need the heavy stones for burning wood and keeping the fire going. You know you're smarter than this Neanderthal who hasn't yet learned to get out of a dark, damp cave, but you're not smart enough to make transporting this heavy stone any easier. Your body aches, and your head hurts. You're too tired to go on, and you're frustrated. You watch as the Neanderthal shoves his stone over the trees you cut down to make a clearing for your hut. You laugh as he trips over the fallen tree trunks, struggling to keep his stone from rolling backward. And then, as you watch the Neanderthal get angrier and angrier, it hits you! If you put tree trunks underneath your stone, you could actually roll the thing along. Not lug, push, or pull, but **roll** it!

So the wheel was invented out of frustration. How many inventions are the direct result of frustration or stress? Creative thought and inventive adaptation just wouldn't exist unless there were differences between what we need, or our goals, and what we perceive we have. As I've stated so many times, everything we think and do is directed to meet our needs. Without stress to alert us to change and grow, we might never have come out of the cave.

We know that stress is ongoing, yet how we choose to deal with it will depend on what skills we have. **Stress does not tell us what to do**; it only tells us to act differently if we want to feel better. If we understand how to make efficient plans, plans that will help us achieve, to go beyond where we are and become frequent risk-takers, then we can practice creating stress. When we create stress to learn more control, we are no longer overwhelmed and ill-equipped when unexpected pressure occurs.

To act more productively when you are motivated, you can learn:

THE EIGHT CRITERIA OF GOOD PLAN MAKING

1. Keep it **simple**.	Begin with something easy. Don't complicate it. Make your plan one small step beyond where you are now.
2. Be **specific**.	Write down the steps you need to take: what, when, where, how, etcetera.
3. Make a **"DO"** plan.	As opposed to a "STOP" plan. Give yourself positive affirmations about what you are starting.
4. Make it **repetitive**.	Make your plan for something you can do each day, or do often.
5. Keep it **independent**.	Your plan should be something you can do without others having to change first.
6. Make it **immediate**.	Your plan should be something you can start right away or very soon; it should be a "now" plan that doesn't require so much time that you take a day off from work to begin.

| 7. **Write** it down. | Make it, and yourself, visible by putting it in black and white. |
| 8. **Skill Build**. | See yourself developing a new, or enhancing an old skill. Don't just problem-solve. |

After you have learned these criteria, you can apply your new skills to making both routine plans and achievement plans. Routine plans include things you do to keep your life comfortable, like making a grocery list, picking up the laundry, calling your mother, or paying the bills on time.

Routine plans keep you organized and caught up with the ongoing necessities of life. They meet needs at a minimal level and don't actually create a feeling of stress. Stress may occur if you **don't** do them, but not in thinking or planning to do them. That is, unless you plan to pay your bills with rubber checks!

Achievement plans are Skill Building actions that go beyond your present comfort range. Thinking of an achievement plan should cause some stress because you could fail. Writing a letter you have been putting off, telling a joke for the first time at the office, or saying "Hi" to a dynamic person you would like to know could be examples of achievement plans.

The stress may be minimal or tremendous. Either way, the action will take you beyond where you are now. I limit achievement plans to three per day, and some days I only have one. If I "chicken out" and don't act, I rewrite the same achievement plan for the next day and keep writing it until I take some action. Sometimes I act by rethinking my wants, my goals, or my plan of action.

Writing this kind of plan causes stress because it creates a difference between internal goals and what we perceive exists. Closing the difference can be pleasurable if we perceive it that way. My good friend, Ed Ford, who understands Skill Development, told me he chose to perceive his contributions to editing this book as challenging as opposed to a pain in the neck. I chose to believe him!

When you make achievement plans to risk moving beyond where you are now, you can start in any area of your life. It is important to develop efficient stress reducing thinking and acting skills. If your need for belonging requires work, start from where you are right now. Perhaps you have the ability to make initial contact with people but aren't comfortable with conversations. It wouldn't help you to begin a plan to become a public speaker and go on the lecture circuit. Your risk-taking might begin with simply learning two new pieces of information from the newspaper and mentioning your newfound knowledge in a discussion. Rethinking process rather than outcome will make your risking easier.

Plan-making and risk-taking have a ripple effect. Each choice you make, each new pathway, will change other pathways. Plan-making itself builds self-confidence and meets most of your needs while you are in the process of thinking out the steps. When you create pathways and put them into use by actually taking the risk, you meet other needs as well. In the above example you have not only reached out to someone and stretched your social limitations, but also learned two new pieces of information and increased your knowledge. Positive feelings result from the actions and lead to an exhilirating response which bolsters your sense of worth and well-being. Mastery of the created stress builds worth which motivates you even further.

If I change one area of my character or behavior, without realizing it, I build the internal confidence to deal with other areas. In the example below, if my plan were to say "Hi" to three people each day, notice the areas of behavior which this simple plan may alter:

THE RIPPLE EFFECT
(adapted from material by Walter Moody)

1. I say "Hi."

2. I have to keep my head up and notice people.

3. I watch what is going on about me.

4. I smile or nod when seeing the person.

5. I feel good when the person replies.

6. I start seeing positives instead of negatives.

7. I start walking more erect with my shoulders back.

8. I notice my dress and grooming.

9. I develop conversation to use after saying "Hi."

10. I look for further involvement.

WhMPAs avoid making waves. Skill Builders generate a ripple effect when they choose to make an achievement plan. Developing confidence requires taking risks. Not much is going to change for the better if you just sit and wait for things to happen. A Skill Builder is not a passive recipient of life. He acts in order to grow, knowing that stress is his friend. He creates it by thinking and then taking risks.

Consider the following lines:

To laugh is to risk appearing the fool
To weep is to risk appearing sentimental
To reach out for another is to risk involvement
To expose feelings is to risk exposing your true self
To play your ideas, your dreams, before the crowd is to
     risk their loss
To love is to risk not being loved in return
To live is to risk dying
To hope is to risk despair
To try is to risk failure
But risk must be taken, because the greatest hazard in
     life is to risk nothing
The person who risks nothing, does nothing,
     has nothing, and is nothing
He may avoid suffering and sorrow, but he simply
     cannot learn, feel, change, grow, love
Chained by his certitudes, he is a slave
He has forfeited freedom
Only a person who risks. . . is free
                  Author Unknown

Risk-taking is opposite to maintaining the status quo. The status quo of WhMPA-Land means looking like, sounding like, and acting like everyone else. It means blending in. You have some rewards when you maintain the status quo, otherwise no one would do it. Your need for belonging and security will be partially met. But choosing to fit ourselves into some group, system, or institution also robs us of our individuality. Where Most People Are is not only a silent majority—it's an invisible majority. WhMPAs think invisible is comfortable. Skill Builders know **Invisible is Miserable**.

I confess to you, when it came to roller skating, I worked hard to stay invisible. It had been fifteen years since I'd skated, but when a group of friends gave me an offer, I chose not to refuse. I was going to take a risk and practice some need-fulfilling actions. Although I've been athletic and stayed active all of my adult life, other sports didn't keep those rolling shoes from getting away from me! My friends were more accomplished, so they scoffed when I pulled on knee pads for my day of skating. They took off while I testily made my first shaky moves. I watched them glide in front of me, as I struggled to keep my balance, aware of the really terrific kids whizzing, turning, and doing tricks in the "fast" lane.

Soon I started to gain more confidence. I caught up with my friends and felt terrific with my progress. We skated along enjoying the beautiful day, feeling how great it was to be sharing this activity.

Then we hit a bank of dirt. I wasn't afraid to fall because my knee pads were protecting me, so I simply let go and fell. My friends, who had looked down on my knee pads, went into all kinds of contortions to avoid falling—hurting themselves by trying not to fall. One pulled a muscle, and the other scraped some skin off her arm. We returned the rented skates since they couldn't go on. Because I risked looking like the novice, my knee pads had prevented a hurtful experience. My lack of self-confidence was an opportunity for creating positive stress that rippled out into Security, Faith, Worth, Freedom, Belonging, Fun, Knowledge, and Health. I had taken the risk, moved beyond where I was and had become visible.

Eventually the success and happiness of Skill Building will promote you from follower to leader. If you successfully adopt the strategy of Skill Building, it means you become the model. To become a model, one must become visible.

Becoming visible begins by rethinking lack of confidence. There are always going to be people "out there" who reject you or your work because their perceptions are different from yours. If you evaluate your world, rethink, and realize that **rejection is not failure, but a difference between what you need and what you perceive someone else wants**, then you will work to be visible and a risk-taker. You will do this because as a Skill Builder you know **you can't control what others are going to think or do**. When you are visible you take the risk of making mistakes. You also get the gain of achieving.

> "The greatest miracle of DNA
> is the capacity to blunder.
> Without it, we would all be
> anaerobic bacteria and there
> would be no music."
> Lewis Thomas

When you evaluate your world and rethink, mistakes won't be mistakes—they will be learning experiences.

It is impossible to eliminate stress. It is desirable to deal with it wisely. You have the tools to begin a strategy to think differently which will make it easier to change what you do.

PART II: BUILDING EFFICIENT ACTIONS

In each of the following chapters, you will find a list of questions preceding the text information. The purpose of these is to stimulate thought about the specific need to be discussed. There are no right or wrong answers. This is **not** a test! You might want to jot down your answers for referral after you complete reading the chapter. In answering these questions, you will begin to discover your present behavior pattern. This awareness will help you to personalize the information as you read it.

CHAPTER SEVEN

SECURITY

"When I own my home, my kids
are grown, and I am financially
secure, then I'll have it made."

WhMPA

"If money is your hope for independence you will never have it.
The only real security that a man
can have in this world is a reserve
of knowledge, experience, and
ability."

Henry Ford

SECURITY

Do you model the skills of strong, happy people?

Do you include others in your plan for support when hard times arrive?

Do you plan time to learn new hobbies or skills?

Do you focus on what you really have control over?

Do you read "How To . . ." books?

Do you ask "How To . . ." questions?

Do you trust other people to meet your needs?

Do you break tasks down into small, simple steps?

Do you work to make money so that you will feel secure?

Do you criticize others?

Do you feel you have control over your negative emotions like angering or depressing?

Do you stay in unfulfilling relationships, jobs, or environments to meet your need for security?

When you are confronted with a stressful situation, do you stop and evaluate what aspects of the situation you cannot control?

Do you depend on others to make decisions that affect your life?

Do you have alternative plans in advance if your first plan should not succeed?

Pretend that I am a genie who can grant you security in an instant. I will let you have whatever you need to make you feel secure, but you only get one wish. Ask for anything your heart desires.

What did you wish for? Was it a home? Money? Power? Perhaps you believe your security will be gained by a prestigious, powerful, solid job? Are you the kind of person who wishes for a mate or an adoring circle of friends to feel secure? Maybe you've felt that if things didn't change so quickly, if you could somehow make time stand still, then you'd feel secure.

If any of those wishes are like yours, you're in the large majority. Most people believe security lies in material possessions, position, money, other people, or maintaining the status quo. Certainly, some sense of well-being will come from obtaining any of these. The problem with such indicators of security is that none is permanent. The price you pay for investing thoughts of security in a house or a job or a mate is that you will never have total control over the emotional investment you make. A job can, and usually does, change. A house can be flooded or destroyed in an earthquake, tornado, or fire. Relationships can deteriorate. If you are preoccupied with holding onto "the good old days," you may find yourself in a constant state of anxiety because no one can control the ever-changing nature of life. All the money, power, or influence cannot prevent change.

A few years ago, I saw Alan, a southern California businessman, who was well-dressed and articulate. He was the epitome of a WhMPA security person. He came to me because he was losing his health, his money, and most of his friends. Alan was caught in a downward spiral he did not understand. "And I earn thirty thousand dollars," he announced, as if his salary were some kind of magic cure that should have given him the security he wanted. I was not overly impressed with such an income from a man who lived in affluent West Los Angeles. Noticing my lack of response, Alan repeated, "Thirty thousand."

I answered, "That's nice."

A puzzled look came over his face. "You don't understand. I make thirty thousand a month!" Now, that was an impressive figure! Yet it was not enough to give Alan, who was spending thirty-three thousand a month on bad investments, ironically misnamed "securities," a sense of security. Not only was he spending more than he earned, Alan's worry over his lifestyle was eating away at his body, and he could not keep people around him. After all, who wants to be with someone who is nervous, sickly, and so preoccupied with his troubles that he is not able to have any fun?

As you can see, Alan's impressive salary and influential job were not earning him enough security. A Skill Builder knows that security depends on something which cannot be taken away, poorly invested, or lost. Alan had yet to learn that **security is gained by developing and possessing the skills to meet all of your internal needs and to take control over your life**. A tall order, you think? Well, I have some tools to help you, as they helped Alan.

Put more security in your life by making a list of what causes you to feel secure. Don't think too much about it—just let the ideas roll off the top of your head. Your list may look something like this:

WHAT MAKES ME FEEL SECURE

> Believing in myself
> Getting married/being married
> My home
> My job
> Friends
> Having bills paid
> A gun
> Safety
> Learning new alternatives
> Gold
> Food
> Being beautiful/handsome
> Good health
> A family
> An inheritance
> A nuclear freeze
> Caring for others
> A blanket

When I give Skill Building seminars, I ask the audience to volunteer their ideas of security. The list above is a sampling of the kind of answers I receive. Although your list may differ, it probably contains items you control, and others over which you have no control.

After you have made your list, circle those items over which you have **complete** control. Using my list as an example, can you circle the first entry? I think so. We have total control over faith in ourselves. Can you circle the second entry? I think not. Even if you find the perfect mate, neither you nor your spouse can control a life accident that might separate you. Marriage cannot be considered absolute security even in the best of circumstances, nor can a home or job, as we saw in the story about Alan. Friends will come and go, and may give you a feeling of momentary security, but they cannot meet your needs indefinitely. You do have total control over paying your bills. A gun may give a sudden rush of power, a feeling of security, but the consequences of making a mistake are devastating. Furthermore, can you always control what other people do when you pull a gun? Safety is an ambiguous feeling that can alter with circumstance. Conversely, you can completely control your ability to learn new alternatives every day of your life no matter what the circumstances.

Going back to the list, gold, considering how the market has fluctuated over the years, can't possibly be controlled by one person. If you circled "receiving an inheritance" as something over which you have control, I'd have to say you'd better be a very good psychic. Who can say for sure how "Uncle Harry" will choose to distribute his fortune? Those who thought they were on the list for the Howard Hughes estate know what I'm talking about! As we go down the list, the only other item you can control is "caring for others."

Determine the difference between what we can control and what we can't. By recognizing how much we may rely on "out there" for our security, we can begin to rethink our choices for meeting our need to feel secure. Security is a need that is **internal**; it cannot be efficiently met by externals. Become conscious of the inefficient pathways you may have chosen, just as you did in Chapter Two; however, this time they specifically apply to the need for security.

First look at the inefficient, out-of-control choices or skills on which people rely for security before they learn to re-think:

INEFFICIENT CHOICES AND SKILLS
TO PRODUCE SECURITY

Possessions
Home
Car
Jewelry
Clothes
Furnishings
Airplane
Boat

Money
Excessive saving
Overworking to earn more
Waiting for an inheritance
Having it made in the future
Putting everything into
"securities" (stocks, bonds)

Status
Job with power
Position where you control
others
Using your title
Maintaining the status quo;
closed to alternatives

People
Making others do what we
want
Treating others as
possessions
Depending on others to meet
our needs

All of these choices could produce a feeling of security. It is a terrific feeling to have things, a good job, and people that you care about. It is just not the most efficient way to feel secure because you can lose any or all of the categories, and by pursuing any of the choices too ardently, you sacrifice fulfillment of your other needs.

I used to play tennis with a dentist who talked constantly about wanting to be an architect. He would sketch and create, read architectural journals, critique new buildings, and talk incessantly about someday going back to college and getting a degree in architecture. He had even sent for books to obtain his contractor's license. But, Dad was a dentist as was Grandpa, so he was destined for the profession. I listened to him many times as he rambled endlessly about his desire to become a creative designer and builder. Having had my fill of his talk, one day I asked him, "If you love it so much, why don't you do something about it?"

"Oh no, I couldn't do that. I would have to go back to school, put in all that time, and who knows, I could fail. Besides, my boy's planning to start dental school in two years, and my wife really enjoys our present lifestyle. I just couldn't ask them to give it all up for me. You know, I'd probably have to give up my membership in the tennis club, too. No, it's too late for all of that."

Sure, there's a payoff in thinking that money will give you everything you need. But after you land that six figure salary and all the status and power that comes with it, even after you acquire all the money you think you want, you will still have many other needs that have to be met. You may feel secure, have faith in yourself, feel that you are a "company man," and belong. You may become a slave to the money or the company and lose your sense of freedom, as my tennis partner did, by choosing comfort over fulfillment.

Money and status can be lost in a recession or depression. Jobs, no matter how secure you may consider yourself, come and go. So can marriages and relationships. The fact is, when things change—and you can count on things changing—a void is created and you can feel insecure. Let me relate a story about life changing abruptly. Here's how it was told to me by my friend Kent:

". . . I'd had my eye on a Porsche for a long time. It didn't matter that a car like that wouldn't fit into my budget; I would have a lot of fun dreaming about sitting behind the wheel of such a beautiful piece of machinery, and dreams don't cost anything. From time to time, I would turn to the used car ads, letting my eyes glance over the descriptions of those lovely impracticalities. Then I'd usually sigh and go back to the sports page. Well, one day last year, I was looking down the Porsche column, and what do you think I see, but an ad for a 1983, black on black, fantasy of fantasies—a Porsche in prime condition. The selling price printed in the paper was fifty dollars! Obviously it was a mistake, but I couldn't keep from dialing the number. A woman answered the phone, I asked her if the advertised Porsche was still for sale. "Oh, yes," she assured me. I told her, oh so coolly, despite the fact that I could hardly get out the words, that I would be right over. Well, it was gorgeous! Not a ding, not a dent—the perfect black beauty! The woman came out— a meek, mild sort of person—and I asked if I could test drive the Porsche. As we went around the block a couple of times, she didn't say a word. I was thinking that this car drives as great as it looks. I'd never actually heard an engine purr!

When we pulled back into the driveway, I kiddingly said, "Listen, I'm not going to haggle over the price—this is definitely worth what you're asking," and I reached into my pocket and pulled out a fifty dollar bill.

To my amazement, she took it saying, "I'll be right back with the registration and pink slip."

I was flabbergasted! When she returned and gave me the documents, I asked her, "Lady, is this car stolen?"

"No."

"Is there something wrong with it that I can't see?"

"No."

"Lady, you know this car is worth over thirty thousand dollars. How could you sell it for fifty?"

"With a satisfied smile she explained, "Well, since you asked . . . this car actually belongs to my husband. About two weeks ago, he ran off with his secretary. I had no idea the two of them were even seeing each other. A few days ago, he sent me a letter with a signed pink slip. He wanted me to sell his car and send them the money! I've always been a dutiful wife, as my husband well knew." Her eyes twinkled, "I'm just doing what he asked."

I love that story! Here was a woman who was probably undergoing great insecurity. Yet she was able to make an achievement plan, take a great risk, and didn't allow herself to be concerned with what others might think. She started building independence skills to take control to meet her needs, including learning to be a fun-maker.

In our mobile society, people average twelve moves a lifetime. If you depend on friends or neighbors to feel secure, you're on pretty shaky ground. Just think about your best friend in grammar school. Is that person in your life now? Don't get me wrong. People are a wonderful pathway to gain belonging, fun, knowledge, and health. Sometimes we can derive feelings of security from others. But we must be conscious that we cannot control or be controlled by people in order to meet our needs for a secure life. When our security is wrapped up with controlling how people think, what they do or how they feel, we will lose every time. Other people not only move away from us geographically, but they grow away from us because either they change, or we change, in ways that no longer make as us compatible. There will be times we won't even be able to exert influence.

Because change is inevitable, maintaining the status quo to feel secure doesn't work. People who make up society are not rigidly fixed in place. What kept the country together in 1941 little resembles what needed in 1968. In the forties, after America had been attacked by a foreign power, the people wanted a unity and patriotism that would preserve national security. But, when America engaged in a war on foreign soil that could not be won, the people wanted to join together to make the government change its policy. It would have been unthinkable to turn against Harry Truman because he sent the A-bomb that ended World War II. Yet Lyndon Johnson didn't run for reelection because his escalation of the war in Viet Nam had turned the people against him. What held true in the "good old days" of the forties didn't apply to the "peace and love movement" of the sixties.

Our society is changing all the time. Change is neither good nor bad, it just is! It is something you can count on, even if you don't know what form it will take. All of the people who invest time, energy, and money in systems and organizations to keep things the way they are, have not kept changes from happening for very long. Despite attempts by some to hold onto the status quo, blacks have benefited from enlightened changes in law, are participating in advanced education, and positions of management and authority. Women have sought a different way of life. Hispanics, Orientals, and other minorities have become more visible. People achieve worth when they grow beyond where they are now. No attempt to keep things the way they are will possibly stop those who are trying to close the distance between what they have and what they need. As Carole King sang, "These are the good old days." Security comes from the skills to be happy here and now.

In order to be happy, it is important to discern the differences between what you think you want and what you *really* want. You've already perceived those things you can't control for your security. Now, concentrate on those things you **can** control, those pathways you can choose to bring more security into your life. Take a piece of paper and make two columns side-by-side. List those things that make you feel insecure in the first column. Again, try to let the thoughts just pop out of your head. Now list those actions you can control which will counter your feeling of insecurity. My sample below will give you a starting point:

INSECURITY	ACTIONS YOU CAN CONTROL TO FEEL SECURE
Being alone	Saying "Hi" first to three people
Being hurt by someone	Calling someone else on the phone and asking how they are
Losing health	Beginning regular exercise
Growing older	Learning a new task or skill
Being laughed at	Learning a joke; being laughed with
Feeling unattractive	Taking a make-up lesson or getting acquainted with a fashion magazine
Being rejected	Rethinking you only have influence over others
Feeling dependent	_____
Failing	_____
Losing a job	_____
Feeling vulnerable	_____
Difficult decisions	_____

When you write your own list, try to determine how each item on the insecurity side will cause a reduction in fulfillment of your other needs. For example, if you lost your job, explore why it feels insecure for you. Perhaps your need for self-worth, belonging, or freedom suffers from not having a job. If those are primary needs that are lost, then you would counter-balance on the secure side by determining a pathway to meet those needs. This exercise will get you started on re-thinking **wants** to **needs,** to put more security into your life. Once you can creatively find alternate pathways to meet your needs, not only will your life begin to change, you will feel a sense of security in taking some control over your choices.

The more skills, the more pathways we can develop to meet our needs efficiently, the less fear we will have. Fear is a feeling that comes from the belief that we are not going to feel okay. Fear is a projection into some future faliure. "I am not going to be all right; I am going to fall flat on my face; something bad is going to happen," are the thoughts that go along with fear. Fear comes more from being stuck in the outcome as opposed to being involved in the process. When a person perceives he isn't able to meet his needs, and doubts he has the know-how to get through a situation efficiently, he fears he will be out-of-control. Fear implies the person who is afraid is giving power to someone "out there" who is going to criticize and judge. **When we rethink from "out there" to ourselves, we realize that no one else has any power over us except for the power we give them**. Eleanor Roosevelt once said, "No one can insult you without your permission." Fear will dissipate as soon as we accept that the power and control result from our choice to give it away.

An important step for enhancing your feeling of security is to perceive the skills you already possess. You are not starting at zero, but you might be surprised to discover you haven't been using all of your potential. My guess is that you have a storehouse of pathways you may have forgotten or allowed to get rusty. I want you to rethink to the past. What did you do that worked successfully to enhance feelings of security? If you feel insecure about being a fun-maker, think back and remember how you successfully had fun as a kid. I'm confident you have at least one memory of an efficient pathway that worked for you, made you feel good, and gave you a sense of security about your actions, feelings, and thoughts. Did you get a group of kids together on a bike ride, plan a picnic, or throw a party? Maybe your successful fun-making was nothing more than taking a walk on the beach. The important thing is that you have resources you can tap to bring more security into your life.

I'm reminded of a friend who felt painfully insecure about any test of physical coordination. Although Mark appeared to be a graceful person, he'd sit on the side lines whenever there were athletic contests like basketball, swimming, softball, or even dancing at a party. He loved sports and music; furthermore, he was knowledgable. Mark watched television, knew all the statistics, and could tell you the specific skills others had which made them successful. However, he never tried to get involved on any level beyond talking. "I'll just step all over your feet," he said whenever his girlfriend tried to coax him onto the dance floor. Or, "I'm not an athlete; I'm a watcher, not a player." His excuses went on and on every time I asked him to participate in a sport. Yet his body was in good shape, and I had a feeling that, if he tried, he would probably be pretty good.

One day, Mark and I spent the afternoon together, sunning and walking on the beach. It was a terrific day and a perfect opportunity to get to know each other better. He confided that he really wanted to be able to play sports like the rest of the guys, but never tried because he felt he'd look stupid.

As we talked and shared confidences, I asked if he had ever played sports or danced before I met him. "Did you play dodgeball, four square, baseball, or even catch, when you were a kid?"

He paused, reflected a moment, then answered, "I played most of those games, but I was terrible! In fact, in most games I'd always be chosen last. Except for handball. In handball, I was okay. You know, as a kid, I was better than okay; I was pretty good! But, the problem was that not too many kids played handball, so I became a spectator." He added, "It's a lot safer being invisible than being criticized and laughed at."

I agreed! We talked a little more about his childhood and successes in other areas. Then it was my turn to share some of the things I had felt insecure about and what I did to over-come them. Near the end of the afternoon, I asked Mark if he wanted to change his feelings about his athletic ability. He laughed, and said, "Sure! Do you have any magic?"

I said, "No magic, but I do have some ideas that have worked for me." I asked him to think back to when he was playing handball. Did he start off skilled and better than the rest of the kids? What did he choose to do to get better, and when he got better, did he still make mistakes? Why did he play handball, and what needs were less fulfilled when he stopped? I kept asking questions to get him to start thinking what skills he could build that he had control over developing now.

By the end of the day, I could see a different look in Mark's eyes. He had started a process so that the fear of "out there" no longer controlled him.

If you're trying to feel more secure and overcome your fears about people, or work, or learning a new technique, it will help greatly to picture how you successfully dealt with a similar situation in your past. If you can't draw on personal experience, you can picture how someone else easily faced a fear that was similar. Human beings are a storehouse of knowledge. Most of us have encyclopedias in our heads, but we have to do some research from time to time. When we don't have a skill or pathway to meet our needs, our minds usually have information on someone else who met his needs efficiently. We can take advantage of the other person's know-how, and model ourselves on his successful behavior. I'll bet you can think of someone right now, at your job or close to you, who has a skill to meet a need efficiently that you would like to possess.

Jim Benepe, a medical doctor in Sheridan, Wyoming, is such a model for me. Jim is always working to build skills to be better at work, fun, and life. He has become a teacher that I and others can learn from by just watching or by being more direct and asking questions. Jim, like all strong people, will always take the time to answer.

The resources available to build skills in all your need areas are only as limited as your imagination. If you feel out-of-control about mechanics repeatedly ripping you off, you can become skilled and secure by taking a class in auto mechanics. If you're insecure about medication your doctor is prescribing, you can do research in any library and ask your doctor informed questions to gain a sense of security about health. If you're like my friend Mark, you can take lessons in any area in which you feel insecure and then practice until you feel competent. Developing skills to take control of your life absolutely benefits the rest of your needs.

To efficiently build security, it is essential to create a strategy for yourself. As I said before, unless you practice rethinking, the old habits will take over, and you will find yourself out-of-control once again. I use a **Skill Building Model** for myself that works, and I offer it to you.

SKILL BUILDING MODEL

1. **Evaluating:** To change, we can decide that what we are now thinking and doing isn't working **enough** to meet our needs. There is a difference between our perceptions of what we need and our environment.

2. **Rethinking:** On two levels: what we are taking in, and what we are going to do differently. The five **areas** are:

A) Out-of-Control to In-Control
B) Wants to Needs
C) Forced to Choice
D) Outcome to Process
E) Negative Stress to Positive Stress

3. **Achieving:** To draw up a simple plan that will take us beyond where we are now and will not cause a loss of any other needs.

4. **Acknowledging:** To feel good about what we are thinking and doing motivates us to do more.

5. **Practicing:** To make a new pathway or skill a habit, it must be an on-going exercise.

A famous coach once said, "Practice doesn't make perfect;

perfect practice makes perfect." You now have a strategy to practice building skills.

You can apply this strategy to your life each day. By learning to change your perceptions of what is happening and then to make a plan, you develop an efficient strategy to be happier. Take, for example, your perception of trust. Have you ever said to yourself, "I'd feel more secure about my friend if I were sure I could trust him?" Or have you ever said to your child, "You'll be in by midnight or I'll ground you for a week!" Because you feel you can't trust him, you are establishing rules and consequences. Your thoughts, actions, or feelings are based in your fear that the person you are trusting won't do the "right thing." If you evaluate and rethink, it will become clear that what is "right" for you may have nothing to do with anyone "out there." Being a Skill Builder, you will rethink your perceptions of others and what you **really** want when you ask others to do "right."

Most likely, you will find that your feelings of insecurity have more to do with expectation than trust in such situations. You may discover that you **expect** your friend to meet your needs by being faithful, honest, punctual, and fair, or you expect your child to meet your needs by being obedient, responsible, and loving. If all of these expectations are attempts to control what others think, do, and feel, the result will be insecurity because you are depending on the uncontrollable behavior of others, rather than working on the skills to take control of what you are thinking and doing.

If I expect things to happen a certain way and they don't, or if I expect someone to think, act, or feel in a particular manner and they don't, I will experience frustration. What I am thinking is not working enough to meet my needs. Stress can work for us or against us, depending on the pathways we choose. Remember, stress is always the motivator that drives us to get our needs met, but the pathways to feel secure under stress may vary greatly in terms of efficiency.

Several years ago, I invested in a cattle feeding program, having been advised by a friend that I could double my money quickly. I lost my shirt. Although I "trusted" my friend and didn't want to think he'd done anything wrong, I was so sure that the two other characters involved in the deal had done me in, I was ready to take them to court. My suspicions and distrust grew; I felt frustrated and began to choose inefficient behaviors like angering, taking revenge, and depressing. At first, I turned on "the unholy trio," blaming them for my feelings of insecurity and loss.

A rethinking process directed me back to my needs and what I could control. Rather than a lengthy court case which would have cost me more money, plus wasted time and emotion trying to "get even," I chose to acknowledge that security is trust in myself. By choosing to place my hopes and money (**I** wrote the check) in the hands of others, I had given them the power to disappoint me. I learned I hadn't taken enough time to investigate the situation thoroughly, and I hadn't educated myself to the consequences. Instead of viewing the situation as a failure, I learned about inefficient pathways. The great lesson was one of the harder realities— strength comes from developing your own skills rather than depending on others. Security comes from having the skills to take control of your life and knowing that no matter what happens, you will continue in the process of building new skills on a daily basis.

CHAPTER EIGHT

FAITH

"If only God would give me a
clear sign! Like making a large
deposit in my name at a Swiss
Bank."
>   Woody Allen—WhMPA Thought

"I think I can— I think I can— I
think I can—I **know** I can! . . ."
>   *The Little Engine That Could*

FAITH

Do you practice thinking of yourself as successful and doing successful things?

Do you have an awareness each day of the things in the world that people did not create?

Do you wake up in the morning and think something like, "It's going to be a great day!"?

Do you think of specific compliments about your physical self while looking in the mirror in the morning?

Do you say positive specific things about yourself to others each day?

Do you have a positive list posted somewhere visible and read it each day?

Do you trust yourself to make the best decisions that you can?

At the end of the day, do you review the day and list the positive things you did?

Do you feel that if you believe strongly enough, your "ship will come in"?

Do you approach each day as a new opportunity to do your best?

Do you believe that improving yourself is more a matter of fate?

Do you accept the status quo because you won't be able to affect things?

Do you work to get others to have the same religion as you do?

Is it important that others know you have faith?

Do you look for positive qualities in members of your family when you see them?

Once I knew a man who truly believed he could take it with him. This elderly gentleman loved money like nothing else in the world. When he thought the end might be in sight, he called in his three best friends to grant him one last request. One friend was a minister, another was an insurance salesman, and the third was a psychologist.

When they gathered around his bed, the elderly man pulled out ninety thousand dollars cash from his mattress, and made his friends swear they would bury the money with him when he died. He doled out thirty thousand to each of them, congratulating himself on how safe his money would be, since he knew each of his friends would check on the other two.

Almost three weeks to the day, the old man passed away. At the funeral parlor the three friends gathered around the coffin, each one with a sheepish look on his face. "You go first," the psychologist said to the minister. The minister pulled out a wad of bills and laid it on the top of the coffin. "Don't bother counting it," the minister said, "I'll tell you up front that the money is short. The church really needed a new roof, and I took ten thousand of his money. I feel so guilty."

The insurance salesman also put a stack of money on top of the coffin. "I feel guilty, too," he told them. "My share is even shorter than yours. I'm embarrassed to admit it, but my uncle needed heart surgery, didn't have enough insurance and asked for my financial help." Red-faced, the salesman confessed, "I'm fifteen thousand short."

"Shame on you both," the psychologist admonished them, "What you've done is just terrible! How could you have betrayed our friend's faith in us to carry out his final request? What you should have done is what I did." He sounded triumphant as he reached into the breast pocket of his new cashmere jacket. "I'm returning the full amount," and he slapped down his **personal check** for thirty thousand dollars.

How many people in this society put their faith in money, friends, institutions, religion, or a number of things that really have nothing to do with faith at all? They may not see their misplaced faith as foolish, yet such people aren't any wiser than the elderly gentleman in my story. In this outcome-oriented society it is easy to mistake what faith is. We are actually taught to believe faith requires some "out there" focus. We are told to have faith **in** something, **in** someone, all for some future good. Most of us don't do as well as the psychologist in the story because we rarely see faith as an INTERNAL need.

Skill Building asks you to rethink everything you think and do. Following this strategy, I will ask you now to reexamine your need for faith, and the ways it can be met efficiently or inefficiently.

Without faith, there is a lack of direction and positive growth in what we think and do. Faith is the opposite of negativity. **Faith is the belief that you are capable of getting what you need, that you are able to achieve**. It is the inborn need to believe, "Yes, I can do it!" Before you took your first step, you had to believe you could do it. Without faith that you could, chances are you wouldn't even have bothered standing up. The first definition in the dictionary sums up this need—belief, trust, confidence. Faith has nothing to do with anything external. Belief, trust, and confidence are thoughts that dwell within us.

There is another aspect to faith which is inborn. No civilization or culture in recorded history has gone without some sort of belief in a greater power. In the Stone Age, people worshipped the stars, rocks, and animals; Druids worshipped trees; Greeks worshipped a pantheon of Gods; Romans worshipped the mystery of the universe; and still today, humans have a need to **believe in some power greater than themselves**. This belief is not the same as religion, although the two ideas often get confused. Faith in a greater power gives a personal feeling of well-being. Although it might feel good to participate in a religious ceremony or attend a religious meeting, the need for faith in a power greater than ourselves does not have to be met in any formal way. Each human being is capable of meeting his need for faith in a greater power by looking up at the stars and contemplating what man did not create, or by recalling surviving a crisis without perceiving why or how.

Like all of the needs, there are efficient and inefficient ways to meet them. First, let's examine some common inefficient pathways or wants. Many people give control of their lives away by choosing to dream about long-range goals. Instead of putting faith in their lives in the here and now, they spend time thinking of the perfect world they expect as a result of the **sacrifices** they are making. "After I build up my business, become financially secure, develop employees I can trust, then I'll be free to take time to make friends and enjoy life. Then it'll be just great," may be a WhMPA speculation. "Then I'll believe in myself, because I'll really be somebody." There are also people who lose so much time intellectualizing, that they don't actually accomplish anything with their lives—I'm not talking about people who actually create great things with their intellectual abilities. I am referring to people who avoid taking any actions by thinking in circles that can lead nowhere. Perhaps you've known a "professional student," a person who's faith in himself was met by attending more classes and acquiring one degree after another. He doesn't have the confidence to step out of the ivory tower to join the working world. People who sacrifice everything for some projected tomorrow, or who over-intellectualize, meet some need for faith, but the cost is great. They lose belonging, some worth, much freedom, fun, and often health in their single-minded pursuit of faith. These people certainly don't gain much security since they are not actively learning new skills in order to meet their other needs.

Another inefficient way to meet the need for faith is by **generalizing**. They say, "I'm going to do something about this weight of mine," yet never really lose a pound. I have a neighbor who complains to any one who will listen about how she regrets never getting her college degree, how she'd like to take a class at the local college, but doesn't know where she'll find the time. As for me, I know I'll get around to cleaning out the garage—one of these days! Generalizing inhibits faith because the goal, even though non-specific, hangs over you as something that feels like failure. Either set an exact time table and do it, or give it up.

There are people who use **religiosity** as an inefficient pathway to meet their need for faith. I believe these people come in five different categories: the person who has found the only true religion and wants everyone else to believe what he believes, the person who blindly follows some religious leader or group, the person who lives only for the "hereafter," the person who believes that he doesn't have to take actions because "God will do it for us," and finally, the person who is "holier-than-thou." All of these people are meeting their need for faith, but they are doing it at great expense to their other needs.

First, the "true believer." If you have never run into the person who has all the answers, who not only thinks he has the only meaningful religious beliefs in the world, but has to force his thinking down the throat of everyone he meets, consider yourself fortunate. This person defines faith for everyone else. And, if you don't happen to believe exactly the way he does, watch out! "You're really in trouble," they say about our differences regarding faith. The truth is these people are the ones who are in trouble, because their insistence on having only one way to believe costs them:

Belonging—Who would want to be friends with someone who was telling them what they must believe?

Knowledge—What new alternatives are they exploring?

Worth–Are they achieving and going beyond their present level of thought?

Freedom—What choices do they give others and themselves?

Can you determine for yourself how they will lose security and fun? They definitely are not in balance with their own needs or those of others. Second, there are the blind followers of groups or individuals. These people are actually saying, "I am so lacking in need fulfillment, so incapable of developing skills to meet my needs, that I must have someone else tell me what to do." Although their actions may look like faith, what the blind followers are doing constitutes the opposite. Faith is the need to believe, "Yes, I can do it." It is the inherent human belief that they can trust themselves and can gain confidence. By doing whatever someone or some group dictates, a person is saying, "Go ahead and take control of my life since you can meet my needs. Now I can **react** instead of work to take control of my own actions." The horrendous tragedy with Jim Jones in Guayana showed how heavy a price is paid for totally trusting others with our faith. Nearly a thousand people died because their religious leader told them there were no positive choices in this world. That was a perfect example of religion without faith.

Third, are the people who live for the "hereafter." They don't have to go to the extreme that the followers of Jim Jones did to be out of balance. I've known several people who have denied almost all of their needs today because they focus all of their thoughts on some hereafter when there will be total need fulfillment. They justify not having any skills to work or to meet people by saying, "I don't need to have a decent place to live or a circle of friends, because I will be compensated for what I don't have on earth when I get to my final destination. There I'll be rewarded for living a religious life." Perhaps they are right, and they may be compensated in some hereafter, but what about the life given them on this planet? Life expectancy gets longer and longer as health and modern medicine improve. Surely, seventy to a hundred years of existence are not meant to be lived just meeting one of eight internal needs. I see such thinking as another way of not taking responsibility for putting balance in our lives.

Is it possible to believe and be in balance? Fulfilling all of our needs in whatever pathway makes us feel happy is what we should hope for. What we **know** is that we are alive now and can think and take actions to take control of our lives. We can improve every situation if we are willing to work to learn new skills.

Next, are people who believe that they don't really need to take responsibility because God will "do it for" them. The kind of person I am referring to says, "So what if that job did not work out; so what if that relationship broke up—it just wasn't meant to be. God must have some other plan for me."

Some time ago, a client, who was very religious, came to me. She was in great pain, had gone from job to job, never working more than a month at any one place, and suffering the insecurity of always being the new employee who was at the lowest end of the pay scale. She had different excuses for each place she left, why "it wasn't meant to be." At one, they gave her more work than she could possibly do; at another, her boss made a pass at her; and at another, her co-workers were prejudiced against her. Her list of excuses and jobs, seemed endless. All of her faith was outside of herself, and it took some rethinking before she could learn that God helps those who help themselves. An old Spanish proverb quotes, "Take what you want," said God, "Take it, and pay for it."

Finally, the "holier-than-thou" type uses an inefficient method to bring faith into his life. He is over-religious, prays without acting, and plays a role in order to impress others. He says, "I am so pious, so religious, no one could possibly be as perfect as I am in how I practice my religion." This individual is really trying to meet his need for belonging and worth by attempting to be the perfect model of righteousness. Unfortunately, the opposite usually happens. He wants others to admire, respect, and consult him. His goal is to get control over others. Yet his attitude is more likely to result in people thinking of him as a jerk, a bore, or a controlling meddler. If he becomes a religious fanatic, people will move away from him in droves. In addition to losing belonging, he generally loses other need fulfillment, especially security, since he focuses only on controlling others, not on gaining control over his own life.

Competitiveness is another factor which is detrimental to meeting our need for faith. What you believe may be very different from what I believe, yet how many of my needs or your needs would be met if we competed for which belief system is "right"? We're back to the "True Believer." "Here is the only answer, the only religion, the only true faith, and I'm going to prove it to you even if it's against your will!" Another old Spanish proverb contributes, "He who is convinced against his will, is not convinced." Such an attitude extends into all sorts of belief systems, from education to morality to politics. Do you recall the presidential candidate who ran on the campaign slogan that a vote for him was what was right for the country? Nonetheless, he lost. We all lose when we try to make our belief system win over the others. By using a questioning approach, we influence ideas, open someone's thinking, or offer information they may not have considered. Instead of saying, "You shouldn't have sex before marriage," you might be more influential by asking, "Have you considered the negative and positive consequences of sex before marriage?" I can give you my point of view if you care to hear it. What is your position?" Acceptance that there are many different belief systems in the world is in itself an act of faith. If you're a terrific model of what you believe, people will come to you and be influenced because they will want what you have.

To be a positive model, a successful Skill Builder chooses to efficiently generate faith in himself. He begins by finding the good, the positive aspects of himself which he already possesses. By recognizing that he already has some tools or skills, he can go on from there to promote an even more positive self-concept. "Humans have a positive side and a negative side, and at each moment, we decide."* In order to have belief, trust, and confidence in yourself, you need to evaluate the good within you. Your entire world expands, and myriads of possibilities open when you approach it with a positive self-concept. When you're thinking negatively, your world is restricted. If I think about failure, if I dwell on those things I don't possess or can't accomplish, suddenly the possibilities for trying look hopeless. Positive thoughts move me forward; negative thoughts drag me down.

*Quoted by Bernard Gunther

Make lists of your attributes. The first list can be a **Positive Physical List**. Start at the very top of your head and work downward, listing only your positive attributes. Even if you don't have any hair, you might find a positive attribute in no longer having to waste money on shampoo! Be specific and thorough. What is positive about your head, forehead, eyebrows, bridge of nose, eyes? Include everything, from your skin tone, to your handsome appearance, to your vision, to how well you can whistle. As you explore your physical attributes, remember that your positive feelings are based on your own beliefs, not on how others may see you or feel about your looks. You may think you have a fabulous smile or a delightful way of winking, even though no one has ever told you so. Even if someone else has said they prefer blue eyes to brown, you may believe your big brown eyes and long lashes are one of your best assets. I'll bet you have some physical abilities you have never before catalogued. It must feel wonderful to still be able to kick that football thirty-five yards, be ambidexterous, or light on your feet when you dance. Perhaps you have a way of walking that is distinctive, or the way you gesture makes a point well. If you feel good about your physical attributes, it shows in the way you hold your head, your posture, and how you appear to others. Conversely, a person with no faith in his physique will deliver the message in a number of external ways by slouching, shuffling, not making eye contact, or in his general appearance. With a sense of faith, you take better care of yourself and pay more attention to your body and how you look.

Now, what's good about you intellectually? Once you've finished your Positive Physical List, consider your **Positive Intellectual List**. You've gained information on a number of subjects. No matter how far you went in school, you can develop more knowledge each day.

Now that Trivial Pursuit has taken the country by storm, the master of trivia might be more in demand than a new Einstein! Consider the way your mind works when you make your Positive List. Are you pleased at how easy it is for you to shut out distractions when you want to concentrate? Do you like how logical you are? Do you feel good about your ability to recall facts or memories? Do you learn something new everyday? If you are an avid reader, you probably have an extensive vocabulary which contributes to faith in your intellectual power. Consider all the creative gifts you possess which are reflections of your intellectual abilities. If you are a creative writer, a painter, a whiz at mathematical puzzles, or lightening with crosswords, these are all indications of intellectual skills. It is amazing how much we take our intellectual abilities for granted in considering faith. John, a friend of mine, is one of the brightest men I've ever known, yet he feels terribly intimidated around people who have advanced degrees. Although he has invented several important new methods for using radio technology, his limited education makes him feel inadequate around those who have been formally trained in his field. Recently, he enrolled in a graduate course at a local university and was astounded that he was not only able to keep up with the regular students, but was delightfully surprised that his life experiences contributed to the course. My friend's face has actually changed from a strained look around his eyes to laugh lines, since he found this new belief in his intellectual abilities.

Speaking of laughter, the next area to inspect is your emotional qualities, and laughter is one. Faith in your feelings will come from recognizing how your emotions successfully meet your needs. The ability to sometimes relate to the way you feel, rather than always relating to what you think, is a positive emotional attribute. If you can say, "I feel hurt when you forget appointments we make," instead of saying, "I think you are a selfish, no-good jerk!" you are using your emotions positively. Empathy, caring, staying calm in the face of stress, are all positive emotional qualities. If you get high from seeing a sunrise or from doing daily routines well, you are proving your success in meeting your needs. If one stressful situation arises after another, and you are capable of staying in-control of your feelings so that you don't make the worst of a bad situation, you have established emotional balance during time of crisis. How spontaneous are you in public? Can you laugh out loud when something is funny? Do you cry at a "tear-jerker"? Do you yell, cheer, or boo at a sports event? If you have an infectuous laugh, your need for belonging will be met since people love to be around someone who knows how to have a good time. Enthusiasm is another emotional attribute that's catching since it helps people feel a natural "high" about life. The chapter on fun discusses ideas of how to promote more positive emotions in your life if your list is lacking. You don't need me to tell you that a short **Positive Emotions List** does not make for a happy or confident life. We don't feel total faith in ourselves if we cannot express our emotions positively. If we hold back continuously, we are not allowing freedom, and our health may eventually suffer.

Now, make up a **Positive Action List**. Here's where you will shine. Think of all your daily activities that you feel have positive qualities, from how well you drive your car to your ability to perform at work, to something as "minor" as your skill at checkers. I think I'd put my good driving record right up near the top of my Positive Action List since I'm really proud of getting only one ticket in the last twenty-two years.

Consider how good a parent, spouse, or friend you are, and list the things you do that make you excel in those areas. As a parent, you might feel skillful in your ability to share in your child's interests, or proud you are consistent, or intuitive about how to help your child through her growing pains. Does it make you feel confident to be a good listener? Do you feel trustworthy about keeping private conversations just between the two of you? Perhaps you are exceptionally good at your work, go out of your way to be responsible, or do things to make the office a more pleasant place. Get specific about the things you do. If you want to list your caring as a sexual partner, that's okay. It may take a little work on your part, but you will feel great to see a list of regular activities you can feel confident about. When you see your positive actions in black and white you will be astounded and recognize what a versatile person you are. You will never have to say, "I just can't do anything; I'll never be able to do that." When you look at a list of those positive things you actually do all the time, it will give you faith in yourself so that you can do even more. If you recall that all your actions started with a first step, it will help you believe you can begin to take a small step now, in a new direction. You have already mastered thousands of actions, from darning a sock to driving a car. Now you can choose to feel strong and in-control because you have a lifetime of actions from which to draw.

The final Positive List is going to help you become conscious of those things that are positive about your **environment**. Everyone has a favorite room, a favorite chair, a favorite picture, or something they keep around them and enjoy. Take a look around and find what is good about your home, your car, or your office. So what if your car is falling apart, and you think it's a pain. There must be something good about it, even if it's only that it runs. Broaden your vision and consider your street, your neighborhood, and your city. Anyone can find what's wrong with them. You find what is **right** with them. Perhaps you live in a run-down neighborhood, but your neighbors are kind and friendly. Maybe your city had a rash of crime, but has the best air in the country. There are hundreds of good points you can list about your country, your world, or your universe, despite what you read in the newspaper or see on the news. The person who is always grouchy about the miserable bunch of people living in his neighborhood, how the country is going to hell, or the world's a mess, says that he has no faith in himself to do well in a miserable world. His belief is, "Why bother to do good or feel good, when everything is so rotten?" A Skill Builder sees that thinking positively, doing good, and feeling good are necessary to get his needs met efficiently, and that's what life is all about. A Skill Builder does not believe life is merely "the six o'clock news" because these are conditions over which he really has little control. Skill Building is recognizing that we **do** have control over thinking positively about the world and the people who live in it. Anne Frank, as a young girl hiding from the Nazis, wrote in her diary in the midst of madness, "At heart I believe people are really good." That belief allowed her to live her short life as fully as possible and gave her faith in herself to reach her potential.

Now that you have drawn up your Positive Lists, make them visible. Post them on the bathroom mirror, the refrigerator door, or anyplace you frequently look.

Below is a partial list of my positive skills, qualities, and surroundings. I have posted my list on my bathroom mirror and, even more visibly, in this text.

PHYSICAL

I have kept my weight at 165, plus or minus five pounds, for the last twenty years.
I work to exercise for ten minutes every day.
I feel coordinated and athletic.
I have small ears.
I have strong arms.

INTELLECTUAL

I read the newspaper or listen to the news almost everyday.
I am able to remember a lot of facts.
I always want to learn more.
I am very organized, which helps me be logical.
I work to listen.
I am knowledgable about what motivates people.

EMOTIONAL

I love to laugh and work to put more fun in my life each day.
I can tell good friends what I feel.
I cry at sad movies.
I want to give and receive love.
I have reduced my negative emotions by practicing rethinking.

ACTIONS

I practice being fair with people.
I am an enthusiastic speaker.
I admit to making mistakes.
I am a creative cook.
I work to not criticize others and instead ask them questions.
In the last two years, I have improved my skills in all facets
    of my golf game.

ENVIRONMENT

My office has a terrific view of the outdoors, with lots of
    trees.
My mattress is the perfect firmness.
My city provides me the choice to do many things.
My city has lots of sunny days.
My car rarely breaks down.

By writing out your lists then posting them, you are reinforcing positive thoughts about yourself and your environment, which will cause your faith beliefs to grow. By making
your lists **available**, you keep them in your daily awareness.
This gives you practice to change, so that you will come to
know yourself in a new, exciting way.

Now that you have more positive belief in what you think,
do, and what you can do, it's time to refine your skills by verbally sharing your good feelings with others. Expressing your
increased faith in yourself will reinforce what you just
learned. Like any other, the skills necessary to meet your
need for faith must be practiced, or they are soon forgotten.

There may be a few problems about how to verbalize your
faith in yourself. Many people hesitate to report their
achievements because they believe they will appear conceited, that no one will really listen, or they may have doubts
about the positive and worry that it might not come out
sounding well. In order not to lose belonging, people sometimes feel more comfortable talking about what is wrong
rather than what is right. Somehow, it seems easier to tell
someone, "I made such a mess at work yesterday," than to
proudly assert, "Wow, did I ever do well with my new com-
puter today!" Think about what feels good for you. Would you

rather be around someone who only reflected his lack of faith in himself, who only told you about the times he messed up? No one enjoys listening to someone's defeats or shortcomings all the time. People are drawn to those who model the positive side of life. You can choose to let people see how positive you are.

If you are general about your positive actions or feelings, you will probably turn people off. Saying, "Am I ever a terrific singer," or "I'm feeling so great," are generalizations that might make people uncomfortable. "I was the best debater in my high school," is the kind of bragging that may cause people to think you are conceited. Can you imagine how you might feel if a friend drew up his Positive Physical List and ran over to your house shouting, "I have the greatest smile in the world!"? You might think he'd lost his marbles. My suggestion is that you get as **specific** as possible when you share positive skills, qualities, or surroundings. Try saying something like, "It felt so good when I learned how to refinish my bedroom dresser. I took a risk and bought a how-to book, sand paper, stain, and varnish. I worked the entire weekend and had a great time learning a new skill." With such news, your friend will be glad for you, since you let him understand what the particulars were to your gaining more confidence in yourself. The more descriptive you can be about achievements, the more people will accept you. When you can accurately tell or write others about the positive things you're doing, they may be enthusiastic for your development. If you don't possess the words to be descriptive, you could get a thesaurus and keep it handy—to help you select new vocabulary to match the new you.

The idea is to become visible. **Invisible is miserable**. When you keep your personality a secret, you stay hidden even from yourself. Skill Building not only requires practice, but it requires reinforcement by revealing who you are. When you share your achievements with others, you **hear** positives as well as tell them. You could wear a button or get a bumper sticker that would identify you as a positive person. Such risk-taking makes you feel better about yourself, increases your faith in who you are, and at the same time meets other needs.

There is a skill you can develop which will bring the positive aspects of meeting faith to your entire family. Once a week, your family can hold a "positive night" around the dinner table. During "positive night" everyone in the family agrees to tell only positive things about one another and their experiences of the day. Each person has a turn to tell the person next to him one positive thing. Specific positive statements are best. "I like your tie, Dad," is not as specific as, "I think the red in your tie contrasts beautifully with your shirt." Initially, your family may feel uncomfortable and balk at the suggestion, saying it's silly or won't do any good. **You** start, and be the model for a few weeks until they see you're not kidding and how good it makes everyone feel. Once they believe enough in themselves to get into it, I guarantee that everyone at the table will feel fantastic. After the first round of positive statements, expand on "positive night" and go around the table once more, having everyone make a positive statement about **themselves**. When the positive statements are **specific**, both the giver and receiver will feel that it's genuine. For example, "I worked very hard to learn how to fix the clutch on my car; I wasn't very confident, but all of a sudden the parts just fit into place. I saved a bundle of money. I did the job myself, and I did it well." How does that make you feel? If the kids say the idea's dumb, stop a moment, **rethink** what you have control over, what needs you want to meet, and what choices you have. Can it be a process, and if stress occurs, do you want to avoid it or make it your friend and grow?

Faith is positive. Therefore, we must view the negative as the absence of faith. Because of our conditioning, our thinking may be automatically negative, especially when it comes to the human tendency to criticize. Some self-criticism is necessary for us to monitor our habits, but being overly critical is the most destructive behavior to efficiently meeting our need for faith.

My friend, Jim Benepe keeps data on his last five rounds of golf. He wants information on fairways hit, sand trap shots, putting, greens in regulation. He believes the more data he has, the better player he will be. If he perceives the data as information to give him **choices** for practice, he will grow. If he gives up and feels badly, then the input is negative.

Excessive, negative criticism from others inhibits growth for everyone, even though the critical person is meeting her need for worth. She implies she is better than you and has the answers to make you the way you "should" be. An example of an extremely judgmental comment is: "Did you notice that outfit Margot was wearing? Her dress showed everything but good taste."

There is no such thing as "constructive criticism" of others—the two words contradict each other. George Carlin has fun with a list of similarly incompatible words: jumbo shrimp, pretty ugly, volunteer army. To this list I add: constructive criticism.

Faith is an internal experience that is reinforced by belief in ourselves. It is trusting and feeling confident about who we are. Criticism, whether of ourselves or others, is usually destructive. By criticizing others, we are attempting to change others to do, feel, or say what we want. The remedy for criticism is acceptance of ourselves and others. When we have faith in our physical appearance, when we accept our faces and bodies in a positive way, we won't have the need to wail to a friend, "Oh, I feel so ugly. I just hate my nose, my mouth is too narrow, and my skin is so sallow." By focusing on other more positive attributes we have, and feeling good about them, we won't need to force others to tell us we look good. Similarly, when we accept Margot's taste in clothes even though it's different from ours, we will not feel the urge to control what Margot is doing to get her to dress the way **we** would like, so that our needs will be met. Reducing our critical comments doesn't mean that we aren't free to try to influence people if our intention is to **give choices**, and not control or put them down. Occasionally someone we know will say something that we don't want to hear. Instead of grabbing them by the collar and shouting, "You don't know what you're talking about!" it might be more effective to ask a question. Instead of constructive criticism which is usually a statement, I employ a "What . . .?", "Can you . . .?", or "Do you . . .?" question. When you ask, "What are you doing to _____?", or "Do you say positive things about_____ ?", or "Do you think_____ is really a good idea?", you are opening channels of communication and choice, so no one's needs will be lost in the process. When you make a **statement**, you are most likely controlling for others changing as opposed to a question where you give or get information. In using questions, you ask the person to make his value judgment about what he is thinking or doing, instead of making it for him.

Here are some efficient ways to increase your faith in a greater power. It feels good to acknowledge that there is more than just us in the universe. Observe the grandeur of creation present everywhere around us. The perfection in a leaf or a flower, the awesome sight of a mountain range, or the stars at night, are moving experiences. We take these phenomenon too much for granted. One way to expand our conscious appreciation of the natural world is to take a "trust walk." In a trust walk, you allow a friend to blindfold you, then lead you through some natural experiences like smelling pine needles, feeling the bark of a tree, or walking barefoot through some lush grass. This opens our other senses to a world we did not create.

Another way to increase our faith in a power greater than ourselves is to let go of the insistence that everything must have a logical reason. Simple acceptance is an act of faith. Think about this: Aspirin has been effective in reducing fever, in stopping arthritic inflammations, and in relieving pain, yet no one really knows exactly how aspirin works. Or, you come into a dark house and turn on the switch without really considering what electricity is. We take aspirin and use electricity, yet we don't comprehend them. We just accept them.

We also don't exactly know how the mind works, yet we use our minds in everything we do. Accept the miracle that is you, and that it is possible for you to make choices which will meet your needs. Have faith in yourself to change your thought system from inefficient, out-of-control behavior to a belief that says,"I can do it!"

Take that leap of faith to believe you can acquire the skills you want; trust yourself to choose good pathways, and have the confidence to rethink.

Now that you're rethinking to put more faith in your life, it's time to put those beliefs into action. Those actions will meet your need for self-worth.

CHAPTER NINE

WORTH

"I don't get mad; I just get even."
WhMPA

"The great end of life is not knowledge, but action."
Thomas Henry Huxley

WORTH

Do you write down new specific ways to achieve something each day?

Do you anger at others?

Do you attempt to change what others do?

Do you try to impress others with your opinions and values?

Do you work to obtain prestige or power?

Do you make general plans, such as: "I want to lose weight." "I want to feel better." "I want to do a better job." "I want to help others.", etcetera?

Do you take risks?

Do you keep pads of paper and pens and pencils around your home?

Do you write out achievement plans for each day?

Do you make plans dependent on only what you do?

Do you make plans to start something?

Do you make plans that are small and simple?

Do you make plans that tell you how many times you will do your new action every day?

Do you make plans that you can practice frequently?

Do you begin your plans within twenty-four hours?

When you are working on an achievement, do you remind yourself that the process is more important than the outcome?

Worth can be summed up in three words: **I LIKE MY-SELF**. Worth is the need for action that comes from faith in ourselves. Once we develop the skills to rethink, "I can do it," then it is necessary to act. If we think, "I can do it," and don't act, our belief will begin to erode and the pictures in our head will remain merely daydreams. Not acting will produce guilt feelings or loss of confidence. We will not feel secure because we will not be creating and practicing new skills. Soon we may question our abilities and use inefficient means to meet our need for worth, such as angering, powering, or criticizing. Our belonging will be strained, and we won't be having much fun. We won't be gaining knowledge in a do-nothing process. To meet the need for worth, we must achieve beyond where we are now, and we must do it every-day. Otherwise, we will find ourselves in the same predica-ment as the lion in the following story.

The King of Beasts felt he wasn't getting enough respect from his jungle subjects. He was really down, frustrated, and disgusted because he couldn't strike terror in the hearts of the other animals as he used to. He felt he had slipped. "Am I not still King? Am I not still tough and mean, and in charge here?" he roared angrily to himself. And with that he shook the burrs from his mane, bared his sharp teeth, and bounded from his den, determined to put worth back into his life. Now who did the lion find right outside his door but the zebra, who didn't even flick his tail at the lion's dust. "I'll show him," thought the lion, throwing back his head and letting loose with a powerful roar that shook the grass on which the zebra was grazing. "Am I not still King of the Jungle?" bellowed the lion.

The zebra was so frightened, his stripes turned white. "Oh, y-y-yes, you are, l-l-lion," the zebra stuttered.

"Harumph!" the lion spat, lifting his head a little higher, but still not feeling enough worth, he went looking for the giraffe. The lion pounced right in front of him, but the giraffe went right on nibbling the leaves of a tree, not even looking down. "You stupid mountain of spots! You're so dumb you haven't enough sense to get out of the rain!" the lion boomed, rattling the tree the giraffe was nibbling. "You know what I could do to you, you stupid stilt-walker! Am I not still King of the Jungle?"

The giraffe trembled until his spots were loose. "Of course you are, lion," the giraffe managed to stammer.

"Ahah!" stormed the lion, raising his mane to its highest heights, but still not feeling enough worth. He wanted to feel stronger and even better about himself. So the lion pranced over to the river bed where he spied the elephant, sloshing mud and water up and down his back. The lion made a wild splash as he struck the water, but the elephant did not bat an eye. "Now I'm really going to feel good," thought the lion, stalking the elephant menacingly. "Elephant, do you know what I just did to those fools who didn't bow down to me? I made jelly out of 'em. You better have the right answer to my question if you know what's good for you!" Then the lion ferociously thundered, "Am I not still King of the Jungle?"

The elephant lazily looked down at the lion as he casually sidled up to him. Before the lion knew what was happening, the elephant had wrapped his trunk around the lion's neck and had him dangling in mid-air. The elephant tossed the lion up, caught him, threw him to the right, threw him to the left, shook him a few times for good measure, flipped him over, and then hurled the King of Beasts about fifty feet down the river!

The humiliated lion raised himself on trembling paws, spewed out a gallon or so of water, and tried to shake the mud out of his mane. Dissheveled and shaken, he managed to call back, "Gee, elephant, just because you don't know the right answer, that's no reason to get so upset!!!

At some time or other, all of us may have used the same sort of inefficient pathway to meet our need for worth. When we don't know how to rethink our wants constructively, it is very tempting to use powering, angering, insisting on winning, or deception to feel strong. Although such pathways succeed with some people, you simply won't be able to scare all of the people all of the time. Also, a high price is paid for such actions. Control of others by force, coercion, bragging or lying, may feel like strength, but in the long-run will weaken us, since no one loves a tyrant. Not only is another more powering person out there to meet your match, but the worth gained is all external, and therefore you are relying on others, rather than learning new skills to generate self-worth from inside.

Even if your actions are not as overt as the lion's, perhaps you have used other, more subtle forms of **powering**. Consider the list below:

Yelling
Physical force
Threatening
Criticizing
Passively-aggressing
Manipulating

All of the angering, controlling actions listed here have a degree of success in producing worth, otherwise no one would ever use them. If you are talking in a way I don't like, saying things I object to, I could get you to stop by yelling or using physical force. By shouting you down or by putting my hand against your mouth, I would get you to be quiet, and so I gain power over you and feel stronger. But what happens to belonging, fun, and freedom by acting this way? Whatever sense of good feeling I might have is momentary. Threatening also has a short life because if you don't go through with the threat, if it is something more drastic than you really intended to do, you feel foolish for having made it in the first place. There is little hope meeting your needs efficiently by threatening, especially if you actually carry out the threat. The same goes for criticizing to get others to change so that you will feel good.

Passive-aggressing and manipulating can be just as abusive as the other powering pathways. I think of the passive-aggressing person as one who angrily takes no action until disaster hits and then looks around at the rubble and shrugs his shoulders saying, "Don't look at me—I didn't do anything." Exactly! The non-action of a passive-aggressing person is a type of indirect control of a situation or person. Instead of telling his wife, "I really hate the ballet, and I would prefer if you went with one of your friends," he doesn't speak up when she mentions she would like to get tickets. When she buys the tickets, makes an appointment with her hairdresser, and spends more than she "should" on a new dress, he still says nothing, silently steaming about how extravagant she is. He may even anger at her about being so frivolous, rather than leveling with her and telling her that he really doesn't want to go. By the night of the performance, he is fidgety and has a headache, a backache, or a toothache. He deliberately arrives home late from the office, but he does get there in time to make the theatre if he hurries. He tells his wife in a calm voice that he is just too sick to go, "But you go ahead without me, at least you can have a good time." So the passively-aggressing person got what he wanted in the first place—to get out of going to the ballet—but this way he made everyone else miserable with his manipulating. He got need fulfillment all right, but he and everyone else lost most of their other needs.

Another inefficient way to bring worth into your life is by insisting on **winning at any cost** or by any method. Here are examples:

> Cheating
> Intimidating
> Having to be at the top
> Over-scheduling
> Competing
> Vicarious worth

Again, these actions all serve a purpose. If we win, no matter what pathways we might choose, we feel good. **Everyone wants to be a winner because society tells us everyone loves a winner**. It's not how you play the game, but how you come out. Right? Wrong, if you're a Skill Builder. By putting the results of the "game" in your mind's eye, you're into outcome rather than process. Can you control what the other person is going to do? Might you play your best game and still lose? You're also putting pressures on yourself that rob you of the fulfillment of fun, knowledge, freedom, and eventually belonging if your pathway for winning is cheating or intimidation.

In a healthful kind of competition, a Skill Builder allows himself to engage in an exercise with someone who matches or surpasses his ability in order to create a challenging experience. If we compete with someone who is as adept or more knowledgable than we, we risk failing, but we also stand to learn something new. Sometimes worth is gained from losing, if in the loss we gain strides from where we were when we began.

For those who don't have enough faith in themselves to take the risk, there is always the vicarious worth gained by identifying with a particular person or group. By identifying with stars, athletes, or other successful people, you can have fun and get some worth. Unfortunately, bragging about the record of your favorite player is not a very dependable way to keep worth in your life, unless you want your worth to depend upon what others do.

Overscheduling is an indirect way of getting worth since the heavily marked up calendar or appointment book can make one appear and feel quite important. Yet he doesn't always feel so great when people anger at him or complain because he can't be depended on for keeping those appointments. This kind of person may look and feel busy and valuable enough to appear to be able to be in two places at once, but his frenzied life is hard on his needs for freedom, belonging, fun, and health.

I've left **deception** for last as an inefficient pathway for worth. It certainly isn't my favorite. How do you like these behaviors?

Bragging
Impressing
Lying
Excuse-making
Exaggerating
Fantasizing

Temporarily, bragging or exaggerating does feel good. Sometimes it's almost irresistable to tell a tall tale, to embellish just a bit for dramatic effect. So we tell one "little white lie" now and then or do a little name-dropping for effect.

Doesn't everybody? Sorry, a Skill Builder does not need excuse-making to justify deceptive behavior in order to put worth in his life. With rethinking, it isn't necessary to fabricate who you are or to irresponsibly fantasize about what you want to be because you are taking control to put worth in your life on a daily basis. Of course, if you do choose embellishing, as a Skill Builder, you don't need to rationalize it through excuse-making. The fulfillment that is lost in other areas when we are caught in one of our "little white lies," or the trust lost in practicing deception, can make any worth gained come crashing down around us. Although instant gratification may be won through these practices, deception is the costliest and least efficient of all the inefficient choices to be made. Lying implies that all of your attention is focused on what other people think of you, how they perceive you, and how you can make them feel about you. Getting worth by trying to make other people see you in an untrue but more flattering light is giving all your power away. **No one else can give you self-worth**. You get it by what **you** do, not what others think.

Even if you manage to get some belonging or fun by deceptive behavior, it is doubtful whether your feeling of worth will be enhanced. Chances are, you'll be wasting time and energy trying to keep up the deception that won you the belonging rather than constructively working to put real worth in your life. Remember, here, as in all of my recommendations, you make the ultimate decision whether or not what you are thinking and doing is efficient. I can only share with you what works for me.

Building the skills for a positive self-concept begins for me by taking risks and daring to achieve. If you feel the stress of not feeling worthy or successful enough, you can begin to put worth in your life by rethinking what success is for you. By practicing Skill Building, you are learning to rethink out-of-control to in-control. If you can perceive success as the process of building skills that you can control, you can have happiness and the feeling of worth continuously. Thinking that success depends on what you earn, your title, or who gives you recognition, takes control away. When you perceive that success is creating as many choices as possible to feel good, you will already have achieved success. The more alternatives you have to achieve, the more in-control and happier you'll be with your life. I've heard that a person who is happy at work smiles going home from the office at the end of the day, while a person who owns a business smiles on the way to the office each day. Skill Builders smile going to work, during the day, and when they come home because they put enough worth in their lives to be happy all of the time, no matter where they are or what the circumstances.

Worth requires achievement. It doesn't have to be a major achievment. If you have never been able to change a tire or the oil in your car, and you master the correct way to do it, that's an achievement.

A bachelor friend of mine, Ron, had never learned how to cook, even though he had lived alone for a long time. He was tired of frozen foods and take-out junk, so for his birthday, he gave himself a gift. He learned which utensils were used in cooking, purchased them, and set about learning how to prepare his own food. It would have been overwhelming for Ron to grab a five pound cookbook and just jump in, so he decided to start in small steps. He wanted to begin with something uncomplicated, something that would give him fairly quick results, and which would not take a great deal of planning or elaborate shopping. He learned how to make a simple omelet. Ron created an easy-to-accomplish alternative pathway to feeling helpless and incompetent. The payoff was that his worth was increased by making an achievement plan and carrying it out in under an hour. He didn't have to wait for next week or the next cooking school beginners' class to put worth in his life. He was so proud of his achievement, it motivated him to experiment with variations. Self-confidence enabled him to attempt more complicated dishes, so Ron was not only able to take better care of himself and meet other needs, but he learned that he could handle cooking disasters without giving up cooking altogether. He didn't begin with Beef Wellington. He started with very small steps, allowing himself to risk making mistakes as he grew. Each day, he took himself one step beyond where he was the day before. "The journey of a thousand miles begins with the first step," an ancient saying goes. Ron's journey has taken him so far, he's having a formal dinner party for twelve at his house next month. Pretty good for a man who only knew how to make an omelet a few months ago!

Risk-taking is the pathway to achievement. Without the decision to move beyond where you are now by attempting new tasks, you will not be able to put more worth into your life. Consider the decisions WhMPAs make when faced with the stress of feeling lack of worth. Suppose a WhMPA played a game of tennis, and everything went wrong. He missed his serve and hit the ball into the net or out of the court. He forgot his sunglasses and was blinded when looking into the sun. His coordination was off, and he missed easy shots. With inefficient pathways to meet the need for worth, this WhMPA might yell at his opponent, criticize, or threaten never to play again. He might consider cheating the next time or lying about how the game went, perhaps making all sorts of excuses.

A Skill Builder, on the other hand, can make a decision to do some small things to improve the situation, like remembering to bring the necessary sunglasses, concentrating more on the ball, taking a lesson, and practicing. A Skill Builder could look the ball into the racket every time he served, get his racket back every time the ball flew over the net, and turn his shoulders on his backswing. These are things that are under his control to do any time during a tennis game. They are actions that will build worth because he is enhancing skills. He is not only into the outcome of winning for worth, but instead taking control and achieving new skills that will become habits. He is rethinking a more efficient way to build worth. A Skill Builder is not afraid of learning because he knows that he must generate some new information each day and practice new pathways in order to achieve worth and go beyond where he is.

There are small steps each of us could take to improve. Everyone can work on an area where he is in total control of gaining self-worth. Here is a simple comparison for you to begin your rethinking in this process. Remember, even if your area is a simple one, you've got to take some risk or you won't meet your goal for going beyond where you are now.

DAY	DATE	WhMPA-THINKING	SKILL BUILDING THINKING
Mon	10–24	"No one called me, so I'm not going to call them."	"I will reach out and make at least two phone calls today."
Tues	10–25	"People aren't friendly in this town."	"I will smile first at three people today."
Weds	10–26	"There is no one out there for me; all single people are jerky."	"When I see the positive and give, I feel better because I am meeting my needs."

You can see from the contrast that WhMPA-thinking is passive and "out there" where the Skill Building process is active, and directed to those things over which you have control. Each day you can do some improvement on your alternative pathways, and you can feel the satisfaction of achieving those tasks you set for yourself. The outcome has nothing to do with a Skill Builder's good feelings because it isn't the result of the phone call that counts. It is the achievement of reaching out and dialing the number that matters. If you need more belonging in your life, you can also begin with a simple plan. It may be just smiling at a stranger.

In order to rethink success, make a specific achievement plan (see Chapter Six) to put more worth in your life everyday. Remember, this plan must include only actions you can control. As a salesperson, you can decide to make fifteen or twenty calls in one day, but you know you have no control over making fifteen or twenty sales. When making your specific plan, keep in mind those things you have control over and those you don't. In order to understand what you really can control, I have a simple exercise for you to try before you draw up your plan.

Choose one activity from the following list. Then imagine a Martian comes up and asks you to **teach him how** to play the game you chose. You can **use only ten steps** before the Martian disappears. Be as simple and specific as possible in the steps you write out. Remember, your new Martian friend has never heard of the activity and knows nothing about it.

ACTIVITY	*HOW-TO STEPS*
croquet	1.
dancing	
fishing	2.
tennis	
golf	3.
racquetball	
juggling	4.
billiards/pool	
quilting	5.
knitting	
skeet shooting	6.
surfing	
softball	7.
mountain climbing	
swimming	8.
horseshoes	
driving a car	9.
bowling	
	10.

By developing ten clear, simple, specific steps, you will achieve success. Each step will show in a graphic way how one has control over each action. The first step has nothing to do with "out there" or outcome. You can't begin to play croquet by waiting for someone to hand you a mallet or by wondering who will win. You begin by focusing on what you personally must do first. These are the building blocks of worth.

Okay! After completing and studying the exercise, you are able to rethink success and draw up small, controllable steps for achievement. There is one more component to putting worth in your life. Taking a risk means being willing to make mistakes. As I stated before, it means making an effort to go beyond where you are now. It also means becoming visible. I'm going to repeat myself because this idea is so important to being a Skill Builder: **Invisible is miserable.**

Many years ago I took a writing course at UCLA. Our first assignment was to tell everyone that we were writers. The purpose of this assignment was not only to make us conscious of our new commitment to writing, but also to serve as a motivating influence. Can you imagine telling someone you're a writer, and when they ask what you are writing, not being able to say anything? You'd feel pretty foolish, right? So the statement that we were writers would force us to choose whether or not to lie or to start writing. By becoming visible, we would not only think about what we wanted, but we would also think about the way to close the difference between what we wanted and what we had.

Your visibility, in terms of worth, might come by sharing your need for the day with a friend thereby letting others know you are taking steps and making new choices to put more worth in your life. It may mean becoming more vulnerable, exposed, or controversial. Perhaps one of your pathways to gain worth would be volunteering time to your political party or an organization. Becoming visible when your choice does not match the choice of your friends or co-workers may be controversial, but your risk-taking will make you feel good about yourself. You won't be so concerned with anyone else "out there" controlling what you do.

One of the most visible and risky pathways for development of self-worth in adults is through the wonderful process of **parenting**. You say, not always so wonderful?! Well, you're right. Parenting can be a very stressful experience, especially if you think you must control your offspring's behavior.

The parent who sees his twelve year old son as a "problem" because of transgressions against the rules at home or school might think, "If my child would change, my life would be better." That is true, and because it is accurate, most parents will first attempt to change what their child is doing. If the child is getting poor grades and a complaining teacher is sending home descriptive notes of misconduct in class, what would a WhMPA parent do? To maintain or produce a feeling of worth, most parents try behavior mod, rules and consequences, or a combination. "I'll give you ten dollars for every

A," to "If you don't start getting better grades, you won't be allowed to participate in extracurricular activities after school," or "I'll be in your room from seven to eight every night to make sure you study." Such behavior might meet the parents' need for worth, thinking that the child's perform-ance reflects their parenting skills, and also thinking that the child will know who is "the boss." In reality, it is the child who is in-control of this situation. He has managed to get everyone in the house to focus on his "problem." If the child is successful in getting time and attention, such "problem solving" may actually encourage him to get worse grades and make even more trouble. Rather than Mom and Dad having time after dinner to relax and talk together, meeting their needs for belonging and fun, they would be watching over Johnny. They would be checking on him and be in the reward and punishment business, costing everyone some freedom, worth, and faith in one another.

Can you force someone to learn without **internal** motiva-tion? Do people really change and work to grow in a direction where they see minimal benefit?

Skill Builders know that motivating others to **want to change** and **teaching them skills** to help them change is the most efficient process to meet their own needs. One way to accomplish this is through administering rules and positive and negative consequences. When rules and consequences aren't working enough, parents can ask themselves what it is they really want. Worth as a parent, belonging, and fun with their child, might be their answer. They are then able to go beyond where most parents are and use the strategy of Skill Building which means they:

Evaluate who has the stress.

Rethink what they have control over, what needs they want to meet, what are their choices, can it be a process, and what can they learn from their present stresses.

Make an **achievement** plan to change their behavior.

Acknowledge their success.

Keep **practicing** building skills.

With a "time out" period to rethink instead of react, they can intellectually acknowledge where they are at that moment. Perhaps they are angering over the news of their son's grades. Rethinking has taught them that angering is an inefficient pathway to meet their needs. They know they want to meet their needs efficiently in any situation, so they rethink **who it is that has the problem**. Is it my child, or is it me? Is there a difference between what I want and what I have? Parents can choose to solve their problems by working on either "out there" or themselves.

If they choose to change themselves, what are their choices? Experience has taught Skill Builders that they have control over:

a. Demonstrating caring

b. Asking questions

c. Giving alternatives

d. Modeling a successful lifestyle

Skill Builders might first choose concern, friendliness, humor, compliments, or listening as pathways to reach their child. Although a power trip might fulfill some of a parent's needs, Skill Builders are very aware of the long-term results of pathways that can lead to a winning resolution for both parties. Then, Skill Builders can choose to teach their child by asking leading questions rather than by alienating him with criticism. It is important to teach through questioning, but not to control for the answers. For example, do you ask your teacher for help after class? Do you say "Hi" first to kids you don't know? When you study, do you ask yourself questions about what you have read on each page before you turn it? In such a process, there are no "right" or "wrong" answers— it's the method of approach that counts. When the child poses answers, you offer support for good ideas or suggestions of new skills the child can develop to meet his needs. It is important that the child's final decision is his choice alone. Parents can say whether or not they think choice "A" is better than choice "B," making it clear that the final decision and the responsibility for it rests with the child. Finally, Skill Builders are good models to their children by demonstrating the skills they would like them to develop. By being a good listener, they show how to pay better attention to others. By experiencing parental caring, the child will learn there is no need to fight or rebel. The parents' asking pertinent questions helps the child learn to find his own pathways to meet his needs creatively and efficiently. By demonstrating consistency in discussing rules and consequences, and then consistently enforcing negative consequences and rewarding positive actions, the parent is controlling what he can do. **He can always give the consequences, but he can't force the child to follow the rules.** By demonstrating they are in-control of what they think and do, parents will influence rather than force. They can let their child make his own mistakes because they know that the stress of the situation will motivate him to change.

Remember Chapter Three and the need wheels and spokes? The more spokes, the stronger the wheel. No doubt there will be times when parents are not achieving what they want. Find other ways to achieve, and you may not get what you want, but you'll get what you need.

Leaving the comfort of using only rewards and punishment to change others will be risky and produce stress. That's just fine, because now you are motivated! Choose once again to make friends of stress and risk. If you make a value judgment that this thinking will lead to more happiness, like need fulfillment, then you're ready to make an achievement action plan.

Begin by starting where you are right now. Keep your plan **simple**. Try not to think about outcome. Remember, you want to go only one step at a time. If you are going to get **specific**, you must include how, what, where, when, how often, etcetera. Your plan should **never be contingent** on what anyone else is doing. When you think, "I'll be nice and do the right thing if you'll be nice," that is a contingency and gives control to someone else. When you can **start** something new, not just stop a bad habit, you give yourself the chance to learn a new skill. Then, in **practicing**, you acknowledge that you are acting for more worth.

Immediacy is crucial if you want your plan to work well. Did you know that an idea not acted upon within twenty-four hours loses 50% of its action potential? And, if someone procrastinates for seventy-two hours, the chances of doing it will be less than 16%? The point is, if you have an idea to improve your feeling of worth, you had better do it now. By putting it off until tomorrow, the chances of old inefficient choices coming back are very high. Since you have a stress by wanting a change, your mind will automatically produce old stress-reducers like rationalizing, giving up, depressing, accusing others, or whatever pathway worked before you learned to make more efficient choices.

Get in the habit of having **writing materials** everywhere. Even if you don't have the time to act on a plan, if you're stuck in a traffic jam or you're waiting for an appointment, you can write down ideas you can work on later. Keep notepads by your bed in case you get a brainstorm in the middle of the night. All of these ideas can be put to use when you do have the time and place to develop them. Writing is essential because it makes visible your commitment to Skill Building and keeps the idea from getting away.

If you've completed all of these steps, you're in the process of Skill Building. The repeated Skill Building process will become second nature after a while. You won't be stuck as a problem-solver who gets his needs met only some of the time, but who is often out-of-control. Where Most People Are is in a rut about how to put worth in their lives—WhMPAs are preoccupied with what they don't have, can't control, and what other people think about them. A person who can develop new pathways daily knows that self-worth comes from inside. Worth is like water. You have to have it everyday or your self-concept will start to die. Once your self-concept diminishes, all of your other needs suffer as well. The way to keep life full of worth is by achieving, risking, and rethinking.

CHAPTER TEN

FREEDOM

"I **have** to . . . "

WhMPA

"What is freedom? Freedom is
the right to choose: the right to
create for yourself the alternatives of choice. Without the
possibility of choice and the
exercise of choice a man is not a
man but a member, an instrument, a thing."

Archibald MacLeish

FREEDOM

Do you daydream about the past or the future?

Do you pay all your bills on time?

Do you plan your day ahead of time even if the plan is to have fun or rest?

Do you say to others that you are CHOOSING to go to your job, stay in a relationship, or live in your location, when you discuss those topics?

Do you discuss with others their choices as you see them and the positive and negative consequences of those choices?

Do you ask questions when you are around others who you believe know more than you? Are you consistent in what you say and what you do?

Do you list your choices to meet your needs when you feel under stress?

Are you willing to pay the negative consequences for your inefficient choices?

Do you have choices to change everything you do?

Do you use expressions like "have to," "must," "can't," "should," "won't," etcetera?

Do you act compulsively?

Do you tell people you are incompetent when you are inconsistent between what you say and what you do?

When you catch yourself making an excuse, do you stop and identify it as an excuse?

Do you purposefully choose different actions to perform habitual tasks? For example, take a different route to work or alter your morning routine?

You have seen how **faith** is the **thought**, "I can do it," and **worth** comes from the **action** you take as a result of that thought. With freedom, you come to the ability to exercise a choice over what you take in and what you send out. **It is having a choice over how you perceive the world and how you act in it**. The more choices you have to meet your needs, the more free you feel.

Papillon, a popular movie made from a best selling novel, beautifully exemplifies two very different ways the need for freedom can be met. In the movie, Steve McQueen plays a character whose preoccupation was escaping from Devil's Island, the notorious French prison of the nineteenth century. From the moment McQueen arrives at the strict and cruel penitentiary, he spends every waking moment planning his escape. He draws another prisoner, played by Dustin Hoffman, into the plot with him, and together they get caught. The punishment facing each prisoner is several years of solitary confinement, a punishment which ends up killing most other men. Yet McQueen is able to meet his need for freedom by choosing a pathway of creative fantasizing. Despite two horrendous periods confined in a five-by-eight foot windowless cell, with inedible food, tainted water, no plumbing, and without contact with another human being, McQueen makes it. He not only lives through his ordeal, but eventually this character, whose mind and body have been ravaged by time and circumstance, emerges from his cocoon and escapes from the island.

"Papillon" means butterfly in French, and McQueen lives up to that name by the end of the movie.

How Hoffman meets his need for freedom is entirely different. His character makes other decisions while in the confinement of Devil's Island. He reflects a person who chooses to achieve freedom by complying and using the system to the maximum for his well-being while McQueen's character meets his need for freedom by going against the system. Hoffman decided he would not bother anyone after his solitary confinement experience because he felt that "making waves" risked more freedom than he cared to lose. He determined that he could no longer buck the system and devised ways to pad it to make himself valuable.

Although the two chose completely different pathways, both successfully survived a situation which killed most other men. The idea is that each of us has many alternatives in any given situation. We can choose from any number of pathways to meet our need for freedom. There is no "right" or "wrong" choice among all the possibilities open to us. There are only efficient choices, which will give us the **feeling** that we are capable of meeting all our needs, and inefficient choices, which make us believe we are restricted.

The opposite of feeling free is feeling restrained, confined, forced, oppressed, or hindered. In other words, we feel victimized if we feel the loss of freedom in our lives. Our very language implies that in order for us to feel free, our environment must supply freedom for us. Such words as restricted, restrained, confined, forced, oppressed, or hindered, suggest that there is something "out there" restricting or oppressing us. It is a common idea that all people this side of the Iron Curtain are free while the poor souls on the other side are not. Isn't America the "land of the free and the home of the brave"? Common knowledge points to freedom as a political, environmental, or philosophical concept.

The strategy of Skill Building teaches that freedom is internal not external. Freedom does not depend on the law of the land. Consider the repressive policies of a country like Poland, and think of the undeniable pathways to meeting freedom which the Polish people have created through their Solidarity movement. **It is by perceiving that we have choices over input and output that we make ourselves feel free**. If we choose to accept the limited alternatives handed to us by a government, a society, or an organization, we will not be able to take control over our lives.

Because loss of freedom comes from inefficient choices, one should become conscious of some traditional pathways that only work temporarily to give freedom. Initially, I would like you to see how emphasizing outcome, rather than re-thinking to process, robs you of freedom. When you get a Scarlett O'Hara attack—"I'll worry about that tomorrow"—you lose freedom by postponing control of your actions. Instead of finding alternative pathways today, you're putting off until tomorrow what you could be doing right now. Outcome-thinking as, "Maybe it'll just take care of itself," robs you of learning responsible behavior, and costs you the freedom of feeling good about facing a situation and trying new skills.

Procrastination is promoted by fearing that we have only one choice. If you believe there is only one alternative, "Either I paint the whole house, or I paint nothing," the pathway you perceive may be so overwhelming that it makes sense to put it off to a "tomorrow" that never comes. Real freedom is perceiving there are choices in every situation. "I could paint only the bathroom today, and the kitchen tomorrow." "I will need help to paint, so I'll hire a hand." "I could call my friend Jack, spend time with him, and talk while we paint." "I could get the kids to pitch in, and use our work as quality time together to teach them that new song."

Freedom is the feeling we get from the awareness that large goals can be achieved by small steps. **Outcome-thinking** includes being preoccupied with "out there" consequences rather than being involved in one's own actions, one's own process. It is thinking, "What will my boss say if I wear a red tie and red socks?" rather than thinking, "I feel so terrific this morning, I want to wear something bright to celebrate." The consequences of what your boss will think and do might be negative. Can you control what your boss will do? If you do dress conservatively to keep your job, realize that it's your choice. You could look for another job, but your actions tell you it would cost you a bigger price than dressing conservatively each day.

Sometimes outcome-thinking produces **self-denial**. Putting off gratification of most of your needs for meeting one or two is fine for a short while, but if self-denial becomes a lifestyle, your feeling of freedom will suffer. Let's say you've been working hard at your job, really burning the midnight oil and giving up your weekends, all to land a new account. You've stopped going to the gym, missed a few parties, and a weekend of skiing with friends. You're exhausted, but you finally land the account and feel terrific about your business achievement. Now it's time for some new choices—or is it? Do you think of other choices, or do you feel **compelled** to do even more at work? Do you **want** to prove to your boss and colleagues that your success was no fluke and that this performance is only the tip of the iceberg? Does your need for more worth take you out of balance? Besides your job, are there other ways to put worth in your life? If you think you must work and practice self-denial to be happy, versus choosing to work and practice balance, you will feel a loss of freedom.

Many times it is your everyday language that reinforces your belief that you must act in certain ways in order to be happy. Look at the list below and see how many times you use these words:

should	between a rock and a hard spot
they made me	can't
won't	must
compelled	forced
up against a wall	no way
inevitable	uncontrollable
destined	stop
if only they would . . .	if only I had . . .
next week	the facts dictate
established	everyone knows
demand	insist
it's meant to be	addicted
inescapable	unavoidable
I was told	

Do you "have to" do anything, or do you "choose" your thoughts and actions? I could eat hot fudge sundaes for breakfast, lunch, or dinner, and anytime in between. I also love being in good physical shape and weighing around one hundred sixty-five pounds. So, I choose to cut back on those calorically evil indulgences. Am I addicted? Am I practicing self-denial? Am I forced, compelled to stop eating them? Have I lost my freedom? The answer to all of those questions is "No!" I haven't lost anything. In fact, by making responsible choices like allowing myself a sundae one night a week, I can meet all my other needs as well. Remember the ripple effect in Chapter Six? Actually, I am freer when I don't indulge in an action which would reduce my feelings of worth, faith in myself, belonging, and health. I am not denying myself, because I rethink of other ways besides eating hot fudge sundaes to meet my need for fun. I feel good about myself when I make healthful choices. This in turn, helps me to feel free.

Consider the words in the list below and ask yourself how many times you use them:

try	attempt
work on	work toward
look at	think about
experience	feel
learn	want to
wish to	hope
achieve	why
would like	wonder about
want to know	going to
will	in touch with
alternative	enjoy
do	appreciate
decide	choose
I find	I can
seek	play

If you think and speak freely, you will be able to take action that will meet your need for freedom. When your thoughts and statements are, "I wonder how it feels to ski," or "Tell me about your trip to Aspen last year," you are considering making a plan to do something to free yourself. When, in your everyday speech you replace **can't** with **may**, **won't** with **could**, or **stop** with **start**, you make your words motivators to change how you act in all your environments.

Another way many people give up freedom is by assuming they are controlled by others. **If you believe that others have power to restrict or entrap you, you won't feel very free**. People who lend themselves to groups or organizations because they don't feel strong enough to make it on their own also lose freedom.

Finally, there are individuals who give up freedom by thinking that all rules and regulations will be followed to the letter. They don't make responsible choices of their own and thus give freedom away. They rely on the military, a marriage, a cult, or a set of regulations to give them freedom, as if freedom were some external thing that is bestowed. The freedom lost by external reliance is that we don't feel the benefit of making responsible choices for ourselves. Besides, the likelihood of any organization, person, or rule book taking care of us is remote. Even in the military, a soldier can make responsible decisions whether or not to follow the orders he is given. **I choose to perceive rules and regulations as opportunities for making decisions that have negative or positive consequences**. When we allow ourselves to be controlled, we are actually making a decision that the consequences of bending a rule will cost more than following it to the letter.

Just think how much easier it would be for teachers and students if they perceived school rules and regulations in terms of choices with positive and negative consequences.

STUDENT CHOICES	POSITIVE CONSEQUENCES	NEGATIVE CONSEQUENCES
To be on time/to be late	Teacher smiles, says good morning	Get tardy slip, have to go to office
Raise hand/speak without permission	Teacher calls on me, and I stay calm	Teacher angers, I sit at back of class
Complete work/ procrastinate	I learn something, get a feeling of worth	Lose points, grade drops, teacher scolds
TEACHER CHOICES	**POSITIVE CONSEQUENCES**	**NEGATIVE CONSEQUENCES**
Smile at class/act coldly	Feel good about caring, increase probability of belonging	Class may not smile or want to listen
Tell a fun story each day/inhibit fun	Have fun in class each day	Some children may not learn that school can be fun, and you could derive little pleasure from your work

| Prepare a new lesson plan for each day/update infrequently | Feel a sense of achievement about your work | Feel bored about your job |

It seems a lot easier to me to see the positive and negative consequences of our action choices as a better way to live, rather than to think we "must" act a particular way. Situations are rarely "either/or" propositions if we rethink that every action we take is a means to meet our needs. There are laws in society which make it more harmonious and safe for people in general. Those people who break the laws are making a choice to fulfill their needs by living outside the system and will suffer the consequences of their choices if they get caught. It is a freeing action to rethink laws, regulations, and rules as opportunities for learning how to negatively or positively meet our need for freedom.

Another inefficient pathway to meet our need for freedom is **living without concern for others**. People who run away rather than working out compromises, or who act as if they are the only ones in the world who matter, are examples of this category. One television commercial tells us we are the "ME" generation, and many people have chosen this identity as an inefficient pathway to freedom. You may know someone who is totally taken up in self-centered actions to the extent that everything he does, says, or feels is justified with, "That's not my problem," or "Whatever." This person may act rudely, thoughtlessly, and when confronted, turn the responsibility onto the other person, "So, you didn't like my talking about you behind your back? Well, that's not my problem. I was just having a conversation and your name came up." That may be true, but for the freedom to say and do whatever a person feels like, the prices in belonging, worth, fun, and health are high. One who controls others by running away or choosing hurtful actions to be free, is saying much the same thing. When he says, "If you don't change, I'll leave," and then does, he is trying to get you to change for him. A person who accuses another of "driving him to drink," and then turns into an alcoholic, is also controlling for the other person to take the guilt and responsibility for his own destructive behavior. Escapism will eventually cost him losses in all of his other needs. Such actions are loud cries for attention and imply that the person thinks he is more important than the others involved. Although inefficient, these means work enough for the egocentrics to feel successful at times.

Irresponsible behavior has successes. Some people choose either **crazy** or **chronically sick behavior** to meet their need for freedom, as well as belonging, worth, fun, and health. Crazy and other sick behaviors are attention-getters, as I noted earlier. It may feel like freedom to those who choose it since their "sickness" gives them excuses for erratic action that they interpret as being spontaneous and free. To more balanced people such thinking is obviously very confining since it is evident how foolish acting sick really is. If someone acts too crazy too much of the time, he's bound to lose freedom. If someone acts too sick too long, he is apt to become bed-ridden. Not much freedom in these choices!

Another pathway that inefficiently meets the need for freedom is **over-spending**. Splurging on a luxury now and then can be beneficial to feeling free and having fun, but when the spending causes excessive debt, freedom is totally compromised. Although it may feel free to "buy out the store," once the credit cards are extended to their limits, one faces the burden of unmet bills. It amazes me how some people apparently believe credit cards are a gift to use whenever they wish. At eighteen to twenty-one percent interest, they are no gift!

A client, who seemed otherwise reasonable, bragged to me as I was getting to know him, that he was worth nearly fifteen thousand dollars. When I asked what he meant, he pulled out a string of credit cards, tallying up the limit on each of them, boasting that he had spent himself up to the limit. He actually thought that being fifteen thousand dollars in debt made him worth fifteen thousand dollars!

As you saw in the *Papillon* example, **fantasizing** can work for us or against us. When a person deludes herself that she is free, yet actually is only digging herself deeper into a rut, she isn't taking efficient action to bring freedom into her life.

The efficient choices to meet our need for freedom come from understanding those choices we have control over and those choices that are beyond our control. In most cases, human beings have many choices, many alternatives, many pathways to meet their need for freedom. First, consider feelings over which we have no control. There are moments in every lifetime that are totally unpredictable and upsetting—a car accident, the death of a close friend, or a tree falling on your house. Less severely, you could come out of your house to go to work and find two flat tires on your car, your favorite shirt gets mangled in the wash, or you lose a prized possession. Whether major or minor, uncontrollable events happen to all of us regularly. What happens when you meet with one of these casualties? If it's as major as a car accident, you may fear, anger, or depress. If it's something as minor as flat tires, you may have similar feelings, but to a lesser degree. You might kick your tires, swear, or shake your fist. The immediate state resulting from such situations is "pure feeling." After the car accident, you might scream, cry, or act crazy, which if continued may not be efficient to meet your needs. In order to get from pure feeling to efficiently meeting your needs, you can move from an emotional state to a rational state. You can choose to ask yourself questions that will cause you to think, instead of just react to negative feelings. You will begin to move away from emotion by asking yourself questions in the five areas of rethinking:

What do you have control over?

Which needs are you meeting?

What are your choices?

Are you in a process, or working for an outcome?

What can you learn from this present stress?

Now you can move from **pure feeling** to **choice feeling**. Although you may not immediately make efficient choices to meet your needs, within seconds from the onset of pure feeling you are able to respond rationally with a choice feeling. After a relatively short time, you will again be able to choose what you are going to think and then do. This usually occurs after you say or think, "Oh my gosh, what am I going to do?" Although the severity of pure feeling can seem overwhelming at the death of a loved one, a Skill Builder can gain strength from knowing that a pure feeling doesn't last forever.

There are some external conditions that are also out of our control. Birth defects, certain inherited diseases, terminal illnesses, all create situations that effect our freedom. Yet, these conditions still allow exercise of efficient choices to meet all our needs. Even though a person may be born blind, deaf, or otherwise handicapped, he still has ways to bring freedom into his life.

I'll never forget a classmate of mine in grammar school. This boy had polio as a baby, and his legs never developed properly. He used his infirmity to wrap the teachers around his finger and as an excuse for being a thoroughly miserable person to the rest of the kids. One day in history class, our teacher told us that Franklin Roosevelt— one of the most effective and powerful presidents—not only had been crippled by polio, but was so successful in his activities and attitudes that millions never suspected that he was partially paralyzed from the waist down. After hearing that, my classmate started to change, as did the rest of us who knew him. He seemed to try harder at everything he did, and we felt less sorry for him, which made him feel free to do more.

Other conditions out of our control include: the influence of drugs once they're in our body—whether the drugs create allergies, intoxication, or crazy actions. We cannot **think** away chemical reactions, a blow on the head rendering us unconscious or strange for a while, the forceful behavior of a criminal who makes his victim anyone who just happens to wander across his path.

By now you have learned that we are out-of-control regarding the behavior of others. We can only influence people where our freedom is concerned. We can't force people to allow us to feel free. Because we fear losing worth, rather than working at the many alternatives we can develop to feel free, people make the inefficient choices of procrastination, outcome thinking, self-denial, assumption of control by others, external reliance, living without concern for others, playing sick or crazy, overspending, or delusional fantasizing.

In order to clarify those things you have control over, write out these three lists:

1. Have the entire family write out five choices each person had today. For example, going to work, getting dressed, reading the paper. Then discuss what are the positive and negative consequences for their choices.

2. Write out those things you are absolutely sure you have no control over, including any actions, thoughts, or feelings you really believe you have no choices in changing. Then have a close friend or relative go over your list with you to check if you really have no choices in those areas.

3. List your eight needs and then find at least ten different pathways to meet those needs efficiently. When you finish, you
   can discuss with a friend or family member how you can
   choose to meet your needs, regardless of what anyone else
   chooses to do.

Another way to see choices is to learn to brainstorm or free associate. Let your mind race! Get excited! What is it that makes your
heart flutter a little and your pulse quicken?

Make a list like this, thinking of choices you can make to go
beyond the traditional ways you've been behaving.

> hot-air ballooning
> change your hair color or style
> splurge on an expensive meal
> pan for gold
> take a "mental health" day off work
> square dancing
> skip down the street
> learn karate
> fly a kite
> buy a plant or flowers for yourself
> hug a friend
> tell a joke

If you're going to feel freer you must break old, restrictive habits
that don't efficiently meet all your needs, and risk being childlike
sometimes or stretching established modes. If you go to a sporting
event, how does it feel when everyone sings the National Anthem
but you keep silent because you can't sing? Does it feel free? I bet it
would feel great to join in and sing at the top of your lungs! I do, and
believe me, I feel great!

Experience your emotions fully. If you feel like laughing, don't
cover your mouth and hide your face. Throw back your head and
have a belly laugh. People love a good sense of humor. If you feel
like crying at a sad movie, go ahead. Your emotional freedom tells
people that you are a warm, caring person and they will not run
away from such qualities. You will gain belonging, not lose it.
When you love, don't be ashamed of your feelings. You can show
exuberance and love whether it's for another person, a sunset, or a

beautiful painting. If you get enthusiastic about a new activity or discovery, it will not only free you, but other people will feel freer to share their activities and experiences with you. What a great model you will be!

Remember, you're thinking of "START PLANS" and "DO PLANS." You're brainstorming for ideas that can allow you to feel more free and spontaneous. You might benefit if you spent a few more dollars on yourself. Perhaps you spontaneously get the idea to learn more about a subject or begin a new hobby. These ideas may cost you something for lessons or materials, but allow yourself the expense and consider it an investment in your freedom to know and enjoy more.

When I think of investing in freedom, I am reminded of my friend Doug. We were browsing in a local book store, and I was debating whether I wanted to buy Leo Buscaglia's *Love*, when Doug said, "You know you can buy another person's brain for the small price of their book."

You can also invest in freedom by being willing to lose. If you're like most people, you keep the "good stuff"—the china, the crystal, the sterling—behind lock and key or high on a shelf, and you bring it out only once in a month of Sundays. What are you saving them for? Your kids, the company, someone special? Aren't you and your family special? If you're not bringing out Grandmother's handmade quilt because you're afraid it will soil or get worn, well, the lack of use puts it out of your mind entirely. If you're protecting it to remember Grandma, how much more alive she'll seem when you have a frequent reminder of her each time you use the quilt. The same goes for the china, because it never gets used. So what if the worst happens and you break some of it? You'll have the opportunity to go out and hunt for another treasured set to start your own tradition.

Let me share a sad, but humorous story of how I learned a lesson about holding onto a treasure too long. Many years ago, I invited a woman to a small dinner party I was having at home. I had hopes of delighting my guests by serving a very rare bottle of Cabernet Sauvignon which I had been saving for several years. I thought I had prepared everything perfectly, and the table looked elegant and sufficiently impressive. When the guests and my date arrived, I went to get the candles to put the finishing touch on the mood, but found I had forgotten to buy any. I excused myself, telling everyone to make themselves at home while I ran out to the store. I wasn't gone more than ten minutes, but when I returned, all of my guests were drinking a mixture my date had graciously prepared in my absence. She was so pleased with herself for having made everyone "wine coolers"—Seven Up and my rare bottle of Cabernet Sauvignon!!! I could have cried!

So you see, freedom can easily be lost unless you act now. Waiting for it to be given to you or thinking that it will come tomorrow, are not always efficient ways to meet this need.

CHAPTER ELEVEN

BELONGING

"If you give first, then I'll give."
WhMPA

"It is not what you can do for me
to meet my needs, but what I can
do, in a relationship with you, to
meet my needs."

Gary Applegate

BELONGING

Do you have three "off the wall" opening statements that you could use to begin a conversation?

Do you invite friends over to play games like cards or board games, or to work on a house project?

Do you wait for others to approach you?

Do you make other people feel guilty to get what you want?

Do you give the other person what they want to receive when you choose to give to them?

Do you think of what to say when others are speaking?

Do you write short notes to people acknowledging their positive behaviors?

Do you allow for other people to do things the way they want, without interfering, even if you think you know a better way?

Do you get a person's eye color when you meet them?

Do you initiate plans to ask others to do things with you?

Do you ask questions to find out what you have in common with others?

Do you say "Hi" first to others?

Do you give specific compliments to others about the way they look or what they do?

Do you look down or away when you talk to people?

When you are in a restaurant, do you start a conversation with your waiter or waitress?

Even though I may never have seen you, I know that we have one basic thing in common. You and I have the common desire to meet our eight internal needs. It is essential for all of us if we are to be happy. It unites us in a common family. Human beings belong together in "life, liberty, and the pursuit of happiness."

Yet there are many people who do not feel good about their place in the world. For some, belonging is not a need that is met naturally or easily. Although there are "loners," people whose need for belonging is less than others and who gratify their needs in other ways, most individuals require people around them in order to meet not just belonging, but all of their needs.

I believe the reason people are lonely in a world filled with involvement is because they have chosen incorrect thinking. **Most people have the false belief that belonging is controlled by the behavior of others**. When troubles arise in any relationship—neighbors, co-workers, or families—it is most likely because people are waiting for change or a positive approach from "out there." When the approach or change doesn't match the pictures they have in their heads, they say, "I've been rejected." Rejection causes a person to feel a loss of belonging which conveys loneliness.

Rejection, figuratively, can tie your hands behind your back, boggle your mind, and set your feet in concrete. If you perceive yourself about to be rejected by another, or imperfect, and therefore afraid of rejection, you will act on those thoughts. Rejection thoughts stop people from approaching others, from developing new belonging skills in their lives, and cause over-concern about what others are thinking. When the focus is too much on what others are thinking or doing, efficient pathways for belonging are sabotaged. Below is a list of WhMPA thoughts that call for others to change first:

1. Most people are boring.
2. All my bosses have tried to take advantage of me.
3. Marriage means "living happily ever after."
4. Most of the single people out there are jerks or misfits.

5. Love happens to others.

6. Breaking up means pain and loneliness.

7. If only my spouse would change my life would be better.

8. Nobody "out there" really listens.

9. Truth is a thing of the past.

10. Physical or material qualities are "where it's really at."

11. You make me feel the way I do.

12. I feel guilty when I disappoint others.

13. If only my mate would say what he really thinks.

14. Rejection is the worst thing that can happen.

15. Relationships seem like a hassle.

16. It's very important what others think of me.

If "out there" were different, would your life be better? Of course it would. This is exactly why WhMPAs think so. Furthermore, because they **think** that way, they **act** to meet the pictures in their heads. What is the result? Frustration, frustration, frustration! Undoubtedly all of us have been on that lonely, painful pathway.

The difference between feeling good **some** of the time about belonging and feeling good **most** of the time, requires Skill Building. A WhMPA chooses people as his wants. WhPMAs think that other people are the main pathways to meet their need for belonging. A Skill Builder perceives that people and relationships are not ends in themselves, because he realizes that relationships are always in flux, and that it isn't others who determine whether or not he will feel good. A WhMPA's goal is to get others to do what he thinks will fulfill his need. A Skill Builder's goal is to learn to get along with all people, despite the many different perceptions and wants they may have, and to attain happiness despite all of the ups and downs others may go through.

Skill Builders find out that "It's more important what I think of you, than what you think of me." A Skill Builder rethinks from, "If you give first, then I'll give," to "I'll give first because I choose to, and it feels good to give." A Skill Builder takes control over how he demonstrates belonging to others, rather than focusing on how much belonging he is receiving.

I'm not implying that a Skill Builder allows himself to be a doormat. Relationships often mean compromise, but a person is not compromising when his friend is drowning ten feet off shore and he swims out five feet saying, "I'm meeting you halfway." Successful relationships exist when each partner can meet the other's needs. Each of us has control over working to meet our partner's needs. If we totally negate our own needs, the relationship is unbalanced. Such a situation was presented to me by Elizabeth, a very attractive, well-educated woman who invested all of her sense of belonging in a man who she believed totally controlled her life.

Elizabeth felt trapped in a relationship which had gradually deteriorated over a two-year period. At first she was completely frustrated, not knowing how to put life back into the relationship. She dressed well, carried herself gracefully, was open and able to express herself easily. She felt very good about the way she demonstrated caring, read the paper to keep up with current events, and exercised for physical fitness. I believed her when she described what a terrific "catch" she was. Elizabeth made elaborate candlelight dinners, gave professional massages, and was a responsive lover.

I could see Elizabeth had several skills which most lonely people don't have. Therefore, I was somewhat surprised to learn this capable and attractive woman was lonely, even though she was involved with a man she said she was crazy about. Since she had never seen herself as the kind of woman who would be with a really good looking man, she was thrilled that someone so handsome was interested in her. This was her first real relationship since her divorce three years before.

In the beginning things were absolutely fantastic. They never had a fight, not even a disagreement, did everything together, and before long she fell in love. Presently, their relationship had deteriorated to the point that their only contact was once a week when he'd come over and jump in bed with her. Elizabeth was very upset because the same sort of distancing had happened in her marriage, and she truly couldn't figure out what she kept doing wrong. From "the best thing that had ever happened to her," the relationship had become one of neglecting all her friends and interests to wait by the phone in the expectation that her boyfriend would call.

As Elizabeth's story progressed, it became evident that this nice looking, competent woman lacked the confidence to say "no." In every relationship there is a need for some sort of counter-control, some sort of balancing effect to the kind of over-dominance that could lead to exploitation. Even the most altruistic person requires some balance of power. No one person can always be right, always have the last word, always get his way. It's only natural that two people have differences from time to time, and only healthy that the differences be aired constructively. Elizabeth was so afraid that her friend would leave her, she never disagreed, never expressed her wants or needs. She had deferred entirely, first to her husband, and now to her boyfriend. At first these relationships worked, because people love a situation where there are no "hassles." As time went on, however, the men in her life would continue to do whatever served their own needs, while less and less of her needs were met. She never asked for what she wanted, thus allowing others to take advantage of her.

By the time Elizabeth came to see me, she was tired of being so solicitous and not getting her needs met no matter what she did. Her fear of losing her boyfriend had stopped her from taking risks. Despite all her skills, she did not picture herself competent to go out and get someone else if she lost this man. She assiduously avoided any fighting that might lead to rejection. Ironically, she was getting rejected gradually by her boyfriend. Instead of choosing different pathways to bring new people and more belonging into her life, she chose depressing, sitting by the phone and bending over backward to please.

After I helped Elizabeth rethink what it was she really wanted, she began to look differently at rejection. She recognized that all rejection results in the loss of belonging. To retain belonging, she had tried harder and harder to please the men in her life. Now the alternative was to realize and accept that these men didn't want her. Elizabeth learned that she could say, "If you can't appreciate me for who I am, and if I can't express my views with you, then it's time to move on and find someone else." With both men, she had been saying, "I will only be all good things to you. That way you can never reject me." She hadn't given them the choice of seeing her as a regular human being, sometimes good, sometimes not so good, allowing them the chance to honestly take her or leave her. Instead she attempted to control them, as well as giving away control over her own life.

Before I met her, Elizabeth had thought of things she could do if she ended the relationship, like going to social events or joining a dating service. She had even considered a blind date. Yet she didn't take any action. She focused on the belief that she couldn't end this relationship because she couldn't stand to get rejected.

The answer was not problem-solving through different actions. Her real problem was not having thinking skills to meet her needs. I asked her to rethink her needs and all of the wants in her life, until she learned to relate her wants to her needs. Elizabeth quickly learned that it wasn't one particular man she wanted, but it was belonging, fun, worth, and all the other eight needs. It was a revelation when she looked at her present skills over which she had complete control to meet her needs. Whereas some people might struggle saying "Hi," making telephone calls, or telling a joke, Elizabeth was already skillful. Her conversation was interesting, since she read the paper daily. As she practiced these skills, she realized if someone rejected her by not returning her "Hi," she could continue and still say "Hi" first again. Gradually, Elizabeth began to feel better about herself.

By changing her perceptions to "rejection" is all around us, and that she can make it a friend just like any other stress, rejection became an opportunity to achieve. The more she practiced the **Five Areas of Rethinking** to overcome her fear of rejection, the better she felt about herself. I helped her to see that rejection is simply the difference between what she needed and what she had, and now that she has chosen new belonging skills, such a perception is not the end of the world.

No matter how wonderful, caring, and lovable we are, someone will reject us at some time. The Skill Builder's strategy in dealing with rejection is not to run from it, but to use it for his benefit.

As Elizabeth's thoughts of how competent, caring, and valuable she was grew stronger, it became impossible for her to wait by the phone. The **process** of life became more important to her than the **outcome** of having some future relationship. She wanted her needs to be met **now**, not in some half-promised tomorrow.

Determined to no longer sit and wait, Elizabeth confronted her fear and called her boyfriend. She took control over her wants by telling him what she liked and didn't like about their relationship. She did not state her wants with the intent of forcing or manipulating her boyfriend into giving in to her. She told him he could choose to give or not to give to her what she wanted. No matter how her boyfriend reacted, her struggle was a success because she knew she was strong enough to withstand the loss of the relationship.

Since he did not want the same things, the phone call ended with a goodbye. Having become a Skill Builder, Elizabeth congratulated herself on taking the risk to confront her boyfriend and on her ability to accept the fact that the relationship was over. Recognizing her many skills, she saw herself as a terrific candidate for putting more spokes on her wheel of belonging. She left me with some words I'd like to share because they illustrate the difference between a WhMPA and a Skill Builder: "I believe I can meet all of my needs, even if there's no man to love me."

Elizabeth had truly learned that **it is more important what you think of others than what others think of you**. Although her intent in relating to people had been basically sound, her motive of avoiding rejection had created unbalanced relationships. For others, the intent may not be so generous. Are you the sort of person who gives only to get something back? If you are, chances are your relationships are just as unbalanced as Elizabeth's were. In a friendship, a person who does things believing that the recipient of the "gift" or "loan" owes him, is creating a contingency kind of belonging. It's a belonging with strings attached, and often includes guilt-making. We all approach people to meet many of our needs. If the intent is to approach, offer, or act, because it

makes us feel good, the approach is usually mutually beneficial. But to smile at someone to get a smile back, is to act to
get someone else to change. If you bring a friend homemade
cookies or a magazine she would enjoy with the thought, "I
wonder what she'll bring me when she comes over," you are
controlling for belonging by trying to get her to meet your
needs in your way, rather than allowing her to demonstrate
belonging in her way.

"Intent," in relating to people is the difference between
efficient and inefficient pathways. There are two basic intention thoughts. The first is to give because it feels good—Skill
Builder's intent. The second is to give to get something in
return—the WhMPA position.

Through rethinking, the Skill Builder chooses to take control and give belonging. Need fulfilling relationships are
those in which both people make a commitment to each other.
The more commitment to a friend, the closer the friendship.
A Skill Builder doesn't wait for the other person to make the
commitment first. If the person is the right friend for you, the
more you put into the relationship the more that person will
want to be around because you are a source of need fulfillment. Would you chase away someone who makes you feel
good? You can determine who you will give this commitment
to, since it would be impossible to give the same level of commitment to twenty "best friends." It is possible to give your
all to one, two, possibly three people at any one time in your
life. Giving that level of belonging to many would mean no
time for anything else.

When we are frustrated by not having enough belonging,
we can choose to Skill Build to bring more people into our
lives, or try inefficient choices. Depressing and paining may
draw people into one's life temporarily, but the price is
terrific!

On the advice of a close friend who was concerned about
her, a recent client called me from the hospital where she had
been admitted after her father's suicide. Camille had an un-
usually close relationship with her father. He had called her
several times each day to talk over his life and ask about his
young grandson. Camille had a happy marriage and a two-
year old boy she loved, yet she felt the most important rela-

tionship she had was with her father. Since his wife's death, her father had gone downhill, suffering from one ailment after another. When he was forced into retirement, he became increasingly depressed and began dropping hints about suicide. One day her father called while Camille was with her brother. This time she believed her father was actually going to carry out his threat. She told her brother to hurry to their father's house while she called the police. Although she raced to see him, her father had already put a gun in his mouth and pulled the trigger in front of her brother and the police.

Camille refused to accept the fact that her father could not have been rescued. She blamed herself, insisting that he would have been saved if only she had arrived in time. Camille was convinced that her father would still be alive if only she could have talked to him.

Camille collapsed. Her anxiety and stress over losing the worth and belonging she had from this intense relationship resulted in acute hysteria. A few weeks after the suicide, she developed physical symptoms from such paining, with headaches, stomach aches, and persistent vomiting, leading to hospitalization.

I visited Camille in the hospital where I found her upset, but coherent. She told me her story, confessing that she may have loved her father even more than her husband and child, and that she was having a very difficult time accepting her father's suicide. When I asked her what she wanted, she said she wanted to accept her father's death, wanted to be physically okay, wanted so very much to again fulfill her responsibilities as a wife and mother, but felt that she was out-of-control and couldn't function. I observed all of the paining and depressing behavior she was doing and explained that her physical reactions to the stress of her father's death could not go away overnight. Her stomach was greatly inflamed as a result of the hysteria, and she would need continued treatment before her body was back to normal. But I assured her she could begin to rethink that there were also actions she could take to feel better emotionally. In order for her to gain back control over her world and give her body a chance to heal, I began asking her some leading questions. "What do you think you lost?" I asked.

"My father," she responded nervously.

"Yes, you lost your father, but more significantly, did you lose a very important pathway to put belonging into your life?"

Camille seemed shocked by my question, but I went on, "I heard from what you said that you felt responsible for your father, that you were the difference between life and death for him. Did that mean that, in addition to giving you a sense of belonging, your relationship also gave you a great deal of worth? Since you were the one in the family he turned to, and you took care of him, do you feel that he let you down when he killed himself?"

Camille burst into tears, confiding that she felt her father's death meant she was incapable of performing the way she should have. She was overcome with feelings of incompetence, but she began to see how much self-worth was in her relationship with her father.

Our session at the hospital was interrupted by a phone call from a caring friend. As my eyes wandered around the hospital room, I saw indications of her involvements scattered throughout. On the windowsill was a large floral arrangement, and gaily colored balloons were tied to the foot of her bed. A plant with a big bow sat on her cart, and greeting cards were taped to the light. In pointing out all of these signs of caring and worth, I reminded her they indicated that a number of people were concerned about her. Although I didn't comment, I felt friends were giving Camille's depressing and paining a great deal of attention. I explained to her that we all have a need to give and receive, a need I call **belonging**, and we meet that need by putting people in our lives. Judging from her hospital room, it looked to me as if Camille were already pretty successful at reaching out to others. I also helped her learn there are things we have control over and those we don't, asking her if she truly believed she could control her father's actions.

Camille recognized she thought she had some control over what her father did, and it was that thought which devastated her. When I helped her realize that we all have choices, and that no person can make someone else choose a pathway he doesn't want to choose, Camille seemed somewhat relieved. As she began to rethink that she did not have actual power over her father's life or death, she started to accept control over her choices to create worth and belonging.

Until then, she had believed worth and belonging came from other people. In that one session she began to discover that there are two kinds of intents. She realized she could give to others, but had no control over others giving back what she needed. In caring for her father she felt worth, but in taking responsibility for his choices she was out-of-control, frustrated, and felt a loss of worth. By learning a new intent of demonstrating caring toward those people who were close to her now, she could have more worth and belonging than she had with her father. Remarkably, Camille found out that she could learn and grow from a terrible situation. The stress of her father's death started to become usable as Camille began to open her mind to the process of rethinking. After a few weeks of new thinking, Camille chose to give up paining and depressing as her pathways to meet her need for belonging. Over a four month period, she internalized the concepts of Skill Building so that happiness really became her choice. On our last visit, she gave me this poem:

> After awhile you learn
> the subtle difference
> between holding a hand
> and chaining a soul.
>
> And you learn
> that love doesn't mean leaning
> and company doesn't mean security.
>
> And you begin to learn
> that kisses aren't contracts
> and presents aren't promises.
>
> And you begin to accept your defeats
> with your head up and your eyes ahead
> with the grace of a woman, strength of a man
> not the grief of a child
> and learn to build all your roads on today
> because tomorrow's ground is too uncertain
> for plans and futures have a way
> of falling down in mid-flight.

After awhile you learn
that even sunshine burns if you ask too much.

So you plant your own garden
and decorate your own soul
instead of waiting for someone
to bring you flowers.

And you learn that you really can endure
that you really are strong
and you really do have worth.

And you learn and you learn
with every goodbye
you learn. . . .

Veronica A. Shoffstall

For Camille, depressing and paining were inefficient pathways to gain belonging. Some people choose powering, guilting, or dishonest relationships to meet their needs. Television shows such as *Dallas*, *Dynasty*, and *Knot's Landing* demonstrate how people relate to powering relationships. Although some may find success in controlling others through tyranny, force, or blackmail, they really lose more than they gain, due to the resentment of their victims. The belonging gained by such behavior is short-lived and shallow. The gains in dishonest relationships are immediate but short-lived. Although extra-marital affairs may provide a sudden surge of belonging, fun, and worth, the price is high in your belonging and other needs at home. In the long run, the gains of inefficient pathways are wiped out by the losses.

An alternative strategy is to evaluate what is working, rethink our input and output, make a simple plan, acknowledge our successes, and keep practicing a Skill Building life style.

If your need for belonging is frustrated because you lack approaching or friendship skills, or feel weak about how you relate to people, here are some exercises which will help. Remember, these are changes in how you act. You will only make successful action changes by first evaluating your world to create a difference and then rethinking input and output.

These exercises are examples of Step Three in the Skill Building Process—Action Plans.

As with all exercises, you must practice before the skills will become a natural part of your behavior. You can congratulate yourself with each exercise since you will be going forward with each one, thus also meeting your need for worth. You will be in the process of learning which will meet your need for knowledge. You will be developing new skills, meeting your need for security, and increasing your faith in yourself by seeing yourself positively. These exercises will also put more fun into your life. With all of these needs met, you're going to achieve a feeling of better health as well.

If you feel you have already developed efficient skills in this area, move on to the next exercise. But, before you choose to move on, may I offer one suggestion? Check yourself out. Some people believe they have good approaching skills and are surprised to discover the opposite is true. I realize that exercises sometimes create negative reactions in people's minds—either they are stupid, silly, won't work, too simplistic, "etcetera, etcetera, etcetera," as "The King of Siam," Yul Brynner, would say. If this is you, I offer no apology but a question. Can you evaluate and rethink enough to try them? If not, feel free to move on to later pages.

If you're a learner, let's start at the beginning! If you feel powerless because of extreme shyness or lack of social contacts, the way to begin to put belonging in your life is by going out where people are.

EXERCISE # 1: Take an hour every day, and that means **every** day of the week, including weekends and holidays, to just mingle with people. You can do it during your lunch hour, on the way home, or after dinner. Schedule this activity into your life as you would any other important daily responsibility. I'll provide a list of places, but as part of the exercise it's your job to find places in your own area which you visit, like:

airports   shopping malls

parks/picnic grounds	public beaches/ pools
zoos	museums
swap meets	sports events
flea market	observatory
historical sites	post office
tours	pet shop
political rallies	fishing piers
public demonstrations	court rooms
city council meetings	tennis courts
bowling alleys	supermarkets

You're changing the pattern of your life in this exercise by learning just to be around people, so I suggest that you determine a different place to go each day. Set up a schedule to visit seven convenient places within the next week and observe how people act and interact in a variety of situations.

By practicing the first exercise, you will acquire new perceptions of people which you can later apply to your own behavior. Even though it is generally believed that communication is verbal, most real communication is nonverbal. Body posture, gesturing, eye contact, and facial expression often speak much louder than words. In fact, studies have shown that in face to face contact only 7% of communication is verbal content, 38% is in tone*, and a whopping 55% is in body language. When you visit the airport, make note of how people behave before they speak to each other. When people say goodbye or greet someone who has just arrived, you will be amazed at how much is said by a movement of the hand or a certain look. You could probably imagine an entire story based on the way one person's body is leaning over the gate, his eyes straining for someone in the crowd, his fingers nervously scratching his head. Now, observe the changes that come over that same body when the person he is waiting for comes into view. His face relaxes into a broad grin, his hand raises to get the other person's attention. It will help to be aware of the messages you communicate nonverbally.

*Many researchers classify tone (paralanguage) in the nonverbal code, thus 93% of communication is nonverbal.

The second exercise helps to develop approaching skills. Again, I suggest starting simply by becoming comfortable with faces and physical appearances. By visiting the same places as in Exercise # 1, or even by practicing this at work, you can progress in your awareness of others and become more comfortable around people.

EXERCISE # 2: Visually analyze three people each day. First attempt to become comfortable with the person's entire body without focusing on any particular part. Describe to yourself what kind of clothing the person is wearing, the type of jewelry, the person's basic physical shape. Next, notice the person's head, his hair (or lack thereof). Move on to his face. Does he have a beard, mustache, distinctive eyebrows, a scar? Now you're ready to concentrate on the person's "middle eye," that spot at the center of a person's forehead on which we can often focus safely. As you grow comfortable looking at this spot, you will find it easier to establish eye color. If you can identify eye color, you are successfully making eye contact. Duration of eye contact depends on what is comfortable for you and the other person. If you find you're having to force your lids open, or if the other party begins to get nervous, you've looked into his eyes long enough! Looking into a person's eyes will be of great help when you've developed conversational skills. It is important to look at the person speaking, so he knows you're listening.

The third exercise is initiating contact by simple gestures, like smiling, nodding, waving, or saying "Hi." When you practice this exercise, you will be taking the risk of approaching someone **first**, instead of waiting for the other person to smile or say hello. For Skill Builders this is an important modeling skill, since being friendly is infectious, causing others to smile back.

EXERCISE # 3: After you are able to identify eye color, then add a smile, a nod of the head, or a simple "Hi." You are not required to stop and engage in conversation. Practice these simple gestures in the mirror before you try them out in public. If you feel not many people smile at you, it's probable that you don't smile first! Get conscious of how your facial expression broadcasts messages to the rest of the world. If you appear happy, you will find others will approach you because a smile meets more needs than a frown or scowl. By adding "Hi" to your happy countenance, you will help people feel good about themselves and comfortable about approaching you. Even if the first person you greet on the street or in a supermarket does not say "Hi" back, it won't be long before your successes far outnumber your failures. Remember, you're learning to rethink rejection and perceive what you have control over thinking and doing.

Smiling and saying "Hi" may seem risky if you're shy, but it has been my experience that most shy people are that way because they're afraid of rejection. In reality, shy people are so busy avoiding eye contact or opening gestures like smiling, they don't give anyone a chance to approach them. If you are shy or feel funny about smiling first, I'll share a beauty contest secret I learned some years ago from a friend who was a candidate for Miss California. She told me that to keep that famous beauty contestant smile throughout those grueling days and nights of the contest, all of the girls rubbed Vaseline on their teeth to enable them to have non-stop grins! She confided that after all that continuous smiling, her face still forms an automatic smile whenever she is in a group of people. She reports that almost everyone smiles back, and most people characterize her as a very happy person. It's a practice that served her well long after her beauty contest days, and it's a practice that can serve you, too. Remember, you are not smiling or initiating a hello just to get smiles returned. If you perform only for the response, you defeat your purpose which is to strengthen your control of approaching skills. You'll find that most successful business people are the initiators. A bank president or maitre d' does not wait for his clients to initiate contact. After you have practiced Exercise # 3 three times a day for a month, it will become an easy, lifelong behavior.

Once these actions have been integrated into your lifestyle, you can start to build conversation skills. It will be easier to move into this step if you prepare. Make a list of easy, comfortable topics of conversation, then rehearse in front of your bathroom mirror. There are several simple opening statements or questions you can use to break the ice. I choose from the five following areas:

1. Something about me.
2. Something about the other person.
3. Something about the immediate environment.
4. Something about the global environment.
5. Something "off the wall."

Let me elaborate:

1. **Something about me:** Be able to make statements about what you did last night or how you are making this day a great day.

2. **Something about the other person:** Notice something distinctive about the person such as a special button, pin, or belt, and remark, "That's an unusual pin. What does it stand for?" You could also ask an open-ended question that might bring out the other person, like, "What do you think about standing in a line this long?", or "What do you know about this movie?"

3. **Something about the immediate environment:** Ask an open-ended question like, "What do you think about the way this room is decorated?", or "What do you like about this restaurant?"

4. **Something about the global environment:** Ask a question of significance about world events, like, "What do you think of the President's budget?", or "What do you think is causing so much violence in the world?"

5. **Something "off the wall":** Last, but not least, I suggest you think up some "off the wall" statements or questions that would cause people to think a conversation with you would be interesting. For example, "What sort of things give you goose bumps?", or "Have you ever wondered what people would look like if they didn't have any eyebrows?" Of course, with "off the wall" questions, you might want to be selective about the time and place!

Back in my college days I used "off the wall" opening statements to initiate conversation wherever I went. It not only brought more belonging into my life, it created a lot of fun. Once while shopping, I noticed an attractive lady in the bakery section of a large supermarket. I had a short debate with myself whether or not to approach her, and my boldness won out over my shyness. I walked up somewhat tentatively, as she was reading the ingredients on a box of cookies. "Excuse me," I said to her, "would you mind if I ask you a question?" She turned a little hesitantly, her big brown eyes flashing as she looked at me.

"Well, no, I don't mind," she answered, a quizzical look on her face.

I felt more confident as I announced, "I'm taking a People Reading course at the University, and one of our assignments this weekend is to go out and read some people. Would you mind if I read you for a while?"

This lovely lady quickly turned back to the cookies, studying the different packages, moved her shopping cart between us, and retorted, "Thank you, but I've already been read." I started to move off feeling rebuffed, and telling myself I had definitely been too "off the wall" for this classy lady, when she flashed a beautiful smile, saying, "Even though I've already been read, it's all right if you'd like to stay and just browse a while!" With that, an informative and enjoyable conversation began. The lesson here is that I had to decide to act on what I wanted and whether to approach or not. It meant taking a risk, but however it had turned out, I would have been successful. By taking risks you will meet spontaneous and interesting people and expand your acquaintances.

EXERCISE # 4: Assuming that identifying eye color and saying "Hi" first have become easy for you, prepare some opening statements or questions with which you are comfortable. Begin by thinking of at least three people you see regularly. It might be the mailman, a co-worker, a bank teller, a friend, or a date. Take the risk of making an opening statement with these individuals each day until you have established a positive habit. It may be a line as simple as, "Where did you get that shirt? It fits you perfectly." Or it could be an environmental or world question, or even an "off the wall" remark. Avoid closed-ended types of questions like: "Where are you from?" "Is this your first time in California?" "Do you like movies?" Closed-ended questions which can be answered with a single syllable like "Yes" or "No" don't do much for initiating conversation.

Even with open-ended questions or statements, some people might be resistant to talking, so you may want to move on to someone else. Some open-ended questions are: "What do you and your best friend do together?" "What do you do for fun?" "What did you do today to make it a good day?" "What is something positive about you?" "How do you exercise?" "Would you like to become famous? For what and why?" Spontaneity will not work for you until this exercise has become a familiar pattern.

Before actually engaging in deep conversation, I suggest you become familiar with some basic tools that keep conversation going. Be aware of the other person's attributes and point them out. Be careful to **mean** it, since insincere compliments can be a turnoff, ruining your chances for good contact. If you choose a specific aspect of the person, make certain the compliment is unique to the conversation. For example, if you are speaking about saving money, it may not be appropriate to suddenly chime in with, "Boy, you look really thin in that blue dress!" It may be more suitable to remark that the person you are talking with had the good sense to buy an economical car, or that she was very wise to teach herself something about auto mechanics to cut down on her bills. Abstract compliments like, "This was a nice lunch!", or "I just love your hair," usually appear empty, not terribly perceptive or appreciative. Comment on how the person **uniquely** arranges her hair, like, "The way you fluffed your hair out on the sides really accentuates your high cheekbones and facial structure." Now, you have let the person know you are aware of the efforts she has made, and how they have enhanced her appearance. When you tell a person, "I thought that your offering to help Jim with his flat tire was a really nice gesture," you are making a personal statement that is meant especially for him. Before you go on to the next exercise, become aware of others' specific, positive aspects, and feel comfortable about pointing them out. Again, a rehearsal list may be helpful.

The next exercise requires some work too, but there is a big payoff, since it meets several other needs besides belonging. In order to hold someone's attention in a conversation, it is necessary to have something to talk about. If you wish to be a good conversationalist, a first step is to obtain interesting information. Being interesting requires some homework nearly everyday. It means getting input. Although you may have a few interesting subjects or topics already, without new sources, you will become boring. No one wants to talk to people who consistently rehash old information or ideas. In fact, many friendships and marriages fade because one or both partners no longer have new material to share. Although conversations in the beginning years seem lively and interesting, over the years they deteriorate by not having enough new things to share. Do you want to go to a party to sit in a corner watching the avocado dip turn brown or, do you prefer to be in the center of things—alive with current, vital information to share?

EXERCISE # 5:   Make a plan **today** to subscribe to a newspaper, magazine, or journal which offers a variety of information not available through your daily experiences. Set your car radio to a talk show or news information station. Watch *Good Morning America* or a similar program on television while you are getting dressed. Buy informative cassettes and listen on your way to work. Place reading materials on your night stand, at your favorite chair, in your purse, lunch bag, the bathroom, or anywhere you might use time to read. Set aside twenty minutes each day for reading. You're going beyond the weather and the ball scores and becoming an interesting conversationalist. You might rehearse some of your newfound knowledge before trying it out on others. I think you will be surprised how little effort is required to become a more informed person. What a kick it will be to open a conversation with an interesting article someone else has read. It may be the beginning of a new, beautiful friendship.

The next step to bringing more belonging into your life is an art in itself. It takes at least two people to make a conversation. With all your skills of approaching: smiling, saying "Hi!" first, complimenting, and your knowledge, a conversation still won't be successful if you monopolize it. The next exercise is designed to help you learn effective listening—important because it demonstrates to others that you are working to meet their needs.

EXERCISE # 6: Make a plan now that tomorrow morning you will initiate a conversation with an open-ended statement or question, and **summarize back** as much as possible what that person says. A summary of five minutes of conversation might take twenty seconds. The object of summarization is to make you aware whether you have really listened or if you've tuned out. It also demonstrates caring. If you can't summarize, then you weren't listening, and you aren't meeting the person's needs efficiently. That means he won't want to be with you as much. Once you learn this exercise, you can tell two people close to you that you are working on summarizing to become a better listener, and ask them to check out your summaries.

By telling other people how you are changing, you make yourself visible, creating a higher likelihood that you will change. At the end of each day, you can summarize what you have learned that day, and **acknowledge** your growth in learning how to communicate with people.

Remember, one way to put belonging and worth into your life is by learning to meet other people's needs. To become a successful conversationalist, it is important to relate well. Therefore, find out what you have in common. Believe me when I say that all human beings have more in common than we realize.

Below is a list of things that almost everyone knows or has an opinion about:

working	inflation	exercise	music
dating	current events	nature	doctors
friendship	television	driving	movies
books	magazines	children	love
shopping	drugs	phoniness	art
food	depression	rejection	politics
entertainment	pets	computers	travel

plants	flowers	restaurants	education
advertising	taxes	law	sports
weather	humor	money	health
government	holidays	weight	fashion
communication	pollution	furniture	parenting

Go back over this list and circle those items you know absolutely nothing about. I mean absolutely nothing! I'll bet you can't find one topic that you're not familiar with at some level. That means you have many, many areas in which you have at least a little in common with everybody else. Seeing how much you already know can help you open your mind to the limitless possibilities available to you for conversation. And, as I stated in the opening of this chapter, you, I, and all human beings share the common basic need to get all of our eight needs met efficiently. With this insight, you are ready to take on the next exercise.

EXERCISE # 7: In the previous list, I provided forty-eight areas we all have in common. Choose at least two and plan to approach two people to discover how you share these topics. Practice opening a specific area; wait for the other's response; ask questions; summarize.

Looking at these areas carefully is an opportunity to get to know yourself better. In searching for a romantic relationship, we sometimes look for love in all the wrong places. How many of us would love to meet Mister, Miss, or Doctor "Right"? You know, a bright, attractive, rich, generous, funny, creative, independent, healthy, secure person who is crazy about us. What a find! But, what would she or he get from being with us? Remember, people stay together for mutual need fulfllment. Therefore, we must always look first at what we have to give before looking at what we can receive. Like attracts like, so look closely at how you act when it comes to money, energy level, intellectual pursuits, emotional feelings, Skill Building strengths, religious preferences, sexual energy, values, and morals. **Then** go out and find someone close to who you really are now.

At this point, you are ready for a significant step to put more belonging in your life. Once you have mastered the exercises above, it's time to plan to do something with another person.

Let me illustrate the next step with a story about an oldtimer, "O.T.", who is a regular at the public golf course I play.

O.T. always had a rough time getting a game. He was a good player, but the other golfers were annoyed by his poor vision—he could never see where his ball landed. Each week as I teed up, I'd see this fella get more and more dejected and more and more reluctant to ask anyone to join him for a round. Who could blame him with all the rejection he was getting! One day while O.T. was practicing putting by himself, Jim, a golfer who used to play with him, rushed up excitedly saying, "Hey, O.T.! I think I found you a partner! This guy's a little older than you, needs help with his game, but he's got eyes like a hawk. You want me to get him?"

The old man actually had tears in his eyes as he answered, "Are you kidding? Why, he may be the golf buddy I've been praying for!"

Jim ran to the clubhouse and returned in a little while with a very old man, but one who seemed spry and active enough for the game. As the two were introduced, you could see both were tickled to death with the new friendship. They shook hands and helped each other to the first tee. I watched as O.T. firmly gripped his club and sent the ball flying. As they left the tee and strode down the fairway, O.T. turned to his new partner, "Tell me," he said, "did you see where my ball went?"

"Sure!" was the loud reply.

"Well, where is it?"

The very old man squinted his hawklike, aged eyes, saying, "I saw it all right! But I just can't **remember** where it went!"

Watching these older gentlemen play golf together is a heart-warming experience for all of us at the course. We saw two lonely people come together to share an activity both enjoyed but couldn't really do without the other.

The last exercise to begin a friendship lets you take control over your need fulfillment by starting a process of asking people to do things you can share. The purpose of this skill is to **actively** pick up the phone and make a contact, rather than to wait, as "O.T." did, for someone to come to you. This step may require rethinking about intent, because the fear of rejection can deter you from taking action. If you want to be a strong Skill Builder, the process of asking has to be an important thought in your head. Doing nothing must be perceived as worse than rejection.

EXERCISE # 8: Make a plan today to ask someone to do something you have in common. Having successfully completed all the other exercises, you have several ideas about mutually enjoyable activities. Your plan need not be elaborate nor cost much money. If you have trouble coming up with affordable ideas, here are a few to consider:

bike riding	fishing
window shopping	free exhibits
buying groceries	garage sales
attending a party	sunbathing
dutchtreat anything	bowling
walking in the park	museums
building a snowman	picnics
attending class together	playing tennis
watching an amateur event	swap meet
	washing your car
visiting 31 flavors and trying all the flavors	

Although this is the final exercise, it is not the end but the beginning. The more activities you share, the stronger your belonging skills become, and the more the friendship will grow. Remember, if you are meeting your needs efficiently by choosing something that is interesting and fun, you will meet the other person's needs as well, since we all share the need for belonging, fun, knowledge, and the freedom we feel when making efficient choices. If you should make a mistake, choosing to take someone to a garage sale who absolutely hates them, you can learn to listen to their choices next time, so that you can compromise on an activity you both enjoy. No matter what, you will have grown when you asked that person to share with you.

Before moving on to maintaining and ending a relationship, I have summarized the action steps necessary to start new relationships. This is a list for strong people who first evaluate, then rethink that they want to get stronger and meet their needs efficiently:

A STRATEGY TO BEGIN A FRIENDSHIP

1. Mingle with people; be where others are.
2. Learn to get eye color.
3. Smile, say "Hi!" first.
4. Prepare open-ended opening questions.
5. Learn to make specific and unique compliments.
6. Acquire papers, books, magazines, cassette tapes, that will make you more informative.
7. Be a good listener.
8. Discover what you have in common with others.
9. Share activities.

Now that you have more self-confidence to put belonging into your life by starting relationships, it is time to become just as confident maintaining them. Although I directly contradict best-selling romance novels and many popular notions, a relationship is not a static thing that lasts forever. Relationships require an openness to change and a desire to accept differences. Each of us has different **pathways** to meet our needs, so there will be differences in all relationships. Conflicts with friends or spouses can be perceived as problems or as opportunities for growth. Until now this chapter has been devoted to establishing relationships—taking all the small action steps leading to initiating new friendships. These steps take work, but the effort it takes to **start** a relationship is nothing compared to the energy it takes to keep one going!

Unfortunately there seems to be a pattern, regardless of the relationship, to "make it legal" and then to "let it die." It's like living in theatre of the absurd, for many of the people who spend so much time and energy "maintaining" a car, home, or business, spend no time maintaining their relationships. Who would think of driving a car for ten years or even one year without having an oil change? What about the filters for the heating and cooling systems in our homes, or the yardwork? People come and go, but the company remains so they say. We have seen over the last decade, however, that companies can also go when turnover or absenteeism result in financial loss. The point is, we live in an "instant" world. We not only have instant tea and microwave dinners, television feeds us daily with instant solutions to major problems. This results in a perception of life being unnaturally easy. Of course, we know better!

A good relationship depends on having things in common; maintaining one also requires commitment. Commitment to a person begins with choosing to share time. The greater commitment made in terms of time spent together, the stronger the feeling of belonging. Of course, there are different kinds of "shared time." It is not so much the **quantity** as the **quality** that is important. I have had many clients who spend hours together, but never "connect," and that is what **quality time** is all about. You can see what I mean the next time you go out for dinner. Look around at people. Eating out is a shared time activity, but you will notice a difference among the groups. Do couples with children talk to each other more or less? Are young couples more involved than old couples? Does dress have anything to do with the amount of interaction occurring? I suspect you will discover none of the above create the difference. You are as likely to find young couples disconnected as old. Families as well, will be different. The key variables are involvement and sharing, not just being there.

I mentioned earlier that boredom can erode the best of relationships, so new input is essential for happiness. Below is the first of three steps that will help a relationship grow:

STEP# 1: Make a list of all the activities you could do with a friend, spouse, or child that would take thirty minutes.

Another list is those things that you can do to bring fun into the relationship. You might include a sport, cooking, playing a game, making a bed, shopping, going out to eat, attending a religious service, or decorating a Christmas tree. You'll be amazed how a pillow fight can create closeness and inject life into a dull relationship. For further suggestions, see the following two lists.

ACTIVITIES FOR WHICH YOU NEED ANOTHER PERSON

tell jokes	magic tricks
take car for repairs	take a class
pairs dancing	pairs skating
intercourse	go swimming
play catch	frisbee
tennis	racquetball
paddle tennis	platform tennis
handball	volleyball
boardgames (backgammon,chess)	badminton
hanging a picture	conversations
watergun fight	sing in a choir
ride a cycle built for two	shuffle board
fly a jet	cut your hair
rub/wash your back	kissing
bowling on the green	hugging
cards (gin rummy, bridge)	body rubs
rob a liquor store (lookout)	wrestle
boxing	sky diving
trust walk	play charades
curling	share trivia
arm/leg wrestling	tickling
move furniture	hide n' seek
cutting & carrying Xmas tree	simon says
spelling bee	scuba dive
listing things to do	snorkeling
water skiing	snow skiing
teach or give information	play hostess

cross-country skiing	tobagganing
snow ball fight	pillow fight
playing ping-pong	playing pool
white water rafting	kats kradle
playing horse	horseshoes
spin the bottle	jacks
pin the tail on the donkey	tug-o-war
relay racing	tag
measuring a room	picnic

ACTIVITIES THAT ARE MORE FUN IF DONE WITH ANOTHER PERSON

cooking	taking a walk
bowling	cleaning house
going out to dinner	doing laundry
jogging	barbecue
going to a sports event	hiking
roller skating	making a bed
visiting the zoo	joining a club
shopping (furniture, clothes)	camping
going to a swap meet	sun bathing
gardening	planning a party
going to a religious service	planning trips
decorating Xmas tree	watching the:
collecting coins	Superbowl,
cleaning attic/garage	Olympics,
taking pictures	Academy Awards,
making a snowman	Elections

By making good things happen on a regular basis, you are "putting money in the bank" for those rainy days when there are tough times.

If you're rethinking ways to strengthen a relationship, one perception which reinforces commitment is to give something you feel like giving, and you know they want. For instance, I could hurry home from work, give Suzy a kiss on the cheek, hand her a fifty dollar bill, rush to the refrigerator, get a cold drink, and plop down in front of the television. I'm thinking of myself as a great guy. Didn't I kiss her when I came in? Didn't I hand her fifty bucks? Actually, few marriages can survive on a quick kiss and an occasional fifty dollar bill. If she wants a solid hug, some attention when I get home, maybe help making dinner so we can share quality time, then that quick kiss may result in quick depressing or quick angering. If Suzy needed me to make some time for her on the weekend to go shopping, my handing her a fifty is not what she really wants.

By learning to be perceptive about the other person's wants and needs, we reinforce our commitment to the relationship. When I come home from work, it's my business to notice other people, and if I'm not sure what is going on, to ask them what they need. You build your own feeling of belonging by giving hugs at the right time, buying gifts that are personal, giving compliments, and spending quality time together.

STEP # 2: Make a list of your best friend's or spouse's wants, and relate those wants to the needs which they meet. Think of alternative ways to meet some of those needs. If you can't come up with a list, ask them to note interests, hobbies, or areas that they enjoy most. Write down the little things you can do that make a difference in how they feel. Will a flower, a note, a phone call, or a little gift make her happy? Do you know a joke which might cheer him? Did you see an article of special interest you want to share? Remember, **your intent is to put belonging in your life by giving, not receiving**. The list below has worked for me.

WHAT TO GIVE A FRIEND TO MAKE ME FEEL GOOD

smile	say "thank you"
give an unexpected kiss	give a warm hug
rub a tired back	clean his garage
apply a cold compress	give a flower

understand a teenager
mail a poem
say you were wrong
tape a love note to mirror
ignore a rude remark
say "I love you" often
use just one parking space
tell him he's wonderful
help him change a tire
buy the wine she likes
clean the house for Mom
play catch with a little boy
laugh at an old joke
encourage a sad person
tell her she's beautiful
laugh when the joke's on you
help her move her piano
take Grandma to lunch
loan a favorite book
tell a bedtime story

remain calm
cut the grass
say "yes"
paint his house
walk with him/her
keep speed
   limit
make the coffee
share a dream
call an old friend
adopt a stray cat
forgive a grudge
visit a shut-in
jog with her
share an umbrella
take kids to zoo
say he was right
explain patiently
pay her bills
send a card

Even in a strong, mutually beneficial friendship, it is vital for both people to have outside interests and activities—something that each can do individually or with someone else, but away from the other party. When one has additional outside sources of achievement, fun, and friends, the relationship is much more one of choice, than dependency. Besides, when you're involved outside, you can bring in new information and experience to keep the relationship alive.

STEP# 3:   Check your relationships to determine if you strike a balance with the other person. Do you depend too much on them for fun or knowledge? Or, are you able to find outside resources yourself? Can you meet your wants away from the other person? What are some of your methods of bringing knowledge, fun, security, and more belonging into your life and the relationship?

Make lists of those environments where you are successfully meeting your needs and those which need improvement. Make an achievement plan to change. Make sure your plan meets all eight criteria of an efficient plan.

When we have full lives apart from our primary relationship, we are saying both to ourselves and the other person, "I choose to be with you, but if you choose to leave, I will be okay. I don't want you to leave, but I can't control what you do. I can only really control the behavior I choose to meet my needs efficiently."

The benefits of having a full, independent life in addition to a shared life, should be obvious. The personal strengths you bring add to the richness of your time together. If both lack sufficient outside interests and activities, most conversations are limited to problems, laments, or hassles. When there isn't much to talk about, conversation turns to negative complaining or withdrawal. Instead of an enriching relationship, the partnership deteriorates into just the differences between what you have and what you want. Arguing, complaining, and moving apart are inevitable when partners aren't contributing new ideas, experiences, and acquaintances.

It's important, when things are not going well, that you start by thinking of activities you can do together, instead of starting to ventilate problems. You'll communicate more with a positive activity than with a conversation of what needs to be changed.

Two people Skill Building, meeting their needs efficiently in everything they do, will have the strongest possible relationship. If the relationship should not endure, both will have gained from practicing efficient skills and can successfully move on. In the diagram below, you will see the strong and weak positions between two people. Where are you in your relationships? (See diagram next page.)

Just as there are skills to increase belonging in your life, there are skills to deal with differences between us and the people we choose to meet our needs. We can increase hassles and get worth by swearing, name-calling, or angering, or we can act efficiently. The skills I will explain include rethinking from **emotional to rational**, **staying on the issue**, **offering information**, or (and sometimes best), **breaking up**. As Neil

two people moving toward
each other.

moving away to get others
to move toward you.

moving toward others when
they are moving away.

both moving away;
temporarily feels bad
for both.

Sedaka said, "Breaking up is hard to do." I will leave that choice for last.

Before you can reduce hassles, you must be rational and thoughtful. When stressed, you will need time to move from an **emotional state to a rational one**. Try the old adage of "counting ten." When you feel too much negative emotion, make a plan to physically move away from your adversary for a set time. "Harry, I don't like you right now, and I don't feel good about what we are discussing. I'm going to take a walk and try to get rational. I'd like to start talking again in two hours if that's okay with you." **Give yourself the freedom to think of alternative ways to gain control over better choices**

to meet your needs. The stress of the situation will surely motivate you to grow. As long as you set a specific time to start approaching again, your partner won't feel rejected and will also probably use the time to rethink.

During the time apart, realize that people have arguments because each thinks he is right. Will a "right" person give up his position and say that he's wrong? Not likely! Think: How can you both be right? How can you both meet your needs? Will controlling your partner work?

The most frequent reason people move apart is over the issue of control. Who is in charge of the money, kids, vacations, television, and the family lifestyle? By attempting to control your partner, you gain worth when your powering is successful. Rethink, "Do I want the worth I get from winning the argument and controlling my partner or, the belonging I can achieve from compromising? Is there a better way to put worth in my life? A way that doesn't involve controlling others?"

Remember, **change will only occur when you rethink a better way to meet needs**.

After rethinking, you will be more inclined to **stay on the issue** which means you will limit your discussion to the subject at hand. You won't bring up issues left over from last month or last year. You won't put someone on the defensive by criticizing or bringing up inadequacies. You'll be able to stick to the issue because you're in-control of the questions you ask and the statements you make. **You'll believe that the outcome or winning of the argument is not essential for your self-worth**. It will be more important to be in a **process** of give and take discussion. If there is any desired **outcome**, it is conflict resolution for the maintenance of belonging. If you simply must win or end the relationship, you can bet the relationship isn't worth very much. Having to win at any cost makes the other person feel like "the enemy," or you, like "the tyrant." No one enjoys such an unbalanced relationship, and eventually belonging will be lost as mutual respect diminishes.

When you **offer information** about what is not working for you, you are giving others a choice. When you just give advice, you are not really giving choices, but are controlling for the other person changing. If you say, "When you are late for dinner I get upset, and when you are on time, I feel good—**it's your choice**," the key is to really mean it's their choice, not to try to inflict guilt so the other person will change. With this information approach, you won't be reducing the perception of freedom. This is especially true if you communicate your willingness to hear their side and to compromise.

When there are problems, and you decide to move toward a person, there will be predictable results. Either the relationship will improve because you both will change sufficiently to meet each other's needs, or you will realize that you are not able to meet each other's needs after all.

Whatever happens as a result of evaluating and rethinking, the process will always produce a strong position. If you both truly are ending the relationship because you cannot be happy, then your decision will be based on the realization that the majority of your needs can only be fulfilled with other people, and the decision is mutually beneficial. However, if you "end" a relationship as a way to control the other person, as a way to "punish" or get them to change, then there is an ulterior motive which cannot benefit either of you.

When a relationship is so frustrating that nothing improves the hassles, if the other person does not respond to the honest changes in you, then it is time to call it quits.

When it's really over—parted, stopped, fini—make a decision that this particular individual is no longer a pathway to meet your need for belonging. Tell yourself and then tell your friends that your "ex" is no longer to be mentioned in conversation. Take down pictures and momentos of the relationship, so you won't be constantly reminded that it didn't work.

Don't come and go. (At least, not more than five or six times! Nobody's perfect!) Once you decide, stick with your plan to move beyond this person to new pathways and experiences. Stop calling them, and if they call, politely ask them not to call again. Move physically away if the person comes into view. If the memories linger in an apartment or house, you may even choose to move. It is important to see these actions as positive, since you will be moving forward toward new goals, new concepts, new people, perhaps even new physical environments. Ask yourself what needs that particular person fulfilled for you, and make the changes quickly to meet those needs in other ways. It is important not to dwell too long or hard on where you both went wrong because it keeps you from moving forward.

Make a decision to say goodbye to old wants; it is time to deal with your present needs. You are alone now, and it is time to find out what you can do **now** for happiness. Focus on those areas that are not being met efficiently. If you have been building skills during the relationship, you will find that your life is not so bad. You have pathways to put fun, worth, knowledge, faith, and belonging into your life without the other person. Your wagon has not crashed, because you have many spokes in your need-wheels. Make a list of your needs, and assess just how you're meeting them in the area of work, friends, recreation, hobbies, intellectual stimulation, spiritual fulfillment, finances, or at home. Where and when will you write out these new achievement plans? As soon as possible, I hope!

For most people who have just ended a relationship, a great big mistake, and one of the most inefficient choices that can be made, is deciding to be alone. The reason this choice is so inefficient is that the need for belonging never goes away, no matter what the circumstances. The person who chooses to be alone at a time when someone close has moved out of his life only gets lonelier and lonelier. If the loneliness can't be eliminated, most people then select other inefficient behaviors to cope with the uncomfortable feelings. Two examples are substance-abusing and tantrumming. A better choice is finding pathways to replace the lost belonging as soon as possible. You can think of them. Go back to the exercises and your lists. We can always rely on close friends or family to help meet the need for belonging. Many people have found a great feeling of belonging from pets. (Just a word of advice: Don't buy one in a moment of weakness—it's too important and lasting a decision.)

When a person close to us is removed for any reason, the way back to happiness is to choose alternate pathways to replace the involvement we had with that person. That doesn't mean we can rush out and find another spouse or best friend. It takes time, but the process when we rethink, can be fulfilling.

If you are back to square one, that's okay. You already have the skills to start with the first exercise in this chapter. It will be a good re-learning experience. You will discover that your hurt doesn't last forever, and you can be doing something everyday to get back into the world to make new acquaintances. In no time your faith in yourself will be restored, and you will be back on the road to Skill Building.

Ask for help from old friends. Not the I-told-you-so's, but your Skill Building buddies. They will be glad you turned to them for companionship or advice or even to have them fix you up with a blind date. Remember, all relationships are a process, even the beginning of one. Any potential involvement with a new person is apt to feel different at first. You are not alone in your feelings. New skills feel strange to everyone. There is always a beginning even to the most beautiful of friendships, so try to learn how to make those brief uncomfortable new feelings your friend.

A few words about blind dates. For both sexes I recommend making the first meeting for lunch or brunch. There are several reasons for a daytime meeting. For one, a lunch or brunch is far less expensive than an evening date. For another, daylight gives you the opportunity to get a good look at the person. In addition, if you are incompatible you can spend an hour and then excuse yourself without having any further commitment. With lunch, you usually don't have to worry about drugs or alcohol, or inappropriate sexual advances. In an hour of daytime conversation you'll be able to discover whether you care to spend more time together, to start a new relationship, and if not, you gracefully avoid disaster.

It really won't matter if it is a blind date for lunch, an "off the wall" statement at the supermarket, a hello at the water fountain at work, or approaching first while waiting in line. To feel better, you can choose to rethink, and then make an achievement plan to practice a belonging skill. You have choices to practice approaching, maintaining, or successfully ending any relationships.

CHAPTER TWELVE

FUN

"Life is boring, and you're no
fun."

WhMPA

"Laughter is the shortest distance
between two people."

Victor Borge

FUN

Do you depend on others to think of ideas to have fun?

Do you buy new sources of fun (comedy albums, tapes, joke books, magic books, trivia books) for your home?

Do you play games only to win?

Do you practice playing a musical instrument you have already learned how to play?

Do you dance at parties when the music starts?

Do you sing along when you hear your favorite song?

Do you plan games for fun when you give a party?

Do you play word games when you are riding in the car?

Do you ask others what they like to do for fun?

Do you learn some trivia each day and share it with others?

Do you look in the refrigerator when bored?

Do you smile while you talk to people on the phone?

Do you think of things in your job to do for fun?

Do you take classes to learn new fun skills, like tennis or cooking?

Do you write down jokes when you hear them?

Do you learn and perform magic tricks for your friends?

Stop me, if you've heard this one:

A young guy is driving down the highway in his VW "bug." The car is completely filled with penguins! Penguins are crammed into every inch of the car.

A highway patrolman, stopped along the side of the highway, sees this peculiar sight and proceeds to catch up to the VW and wave it over.

"What the heck are you doing with all those penguins?" he impatiently asks the young guy. "Take those penguins to the zoo!"

The young man, not really wanting a ticket, smiles nicely and replies, "Yes, sir!"

Next day, the same VW is barrelling down the same highway with all the penguins again. But this time, each of the penguins is wearing sunglasses! The same highway patrolman sees them, speeds up, and signals for them to stop. Now, the patrolman shakes his head, ready to take the guy and the load of penguins into the station.

He demands, "What's wrong with you? I told you to take those penguins to the zoo!"

The young man politely replies, "Officer, I **did** take them to the zoo. And we had such a good time, today I'm taking them to the beach!"

Did you have fun with that story? I hope it gave you a chuckle or two because the whole idea of a happy life is being able to perceive the fun in the world. Having a sense of humor is based on your skill to cut loose from habitual thinking. It is the ability to be playful with what is customarily thought to be serious. Being able to laugh at yourself, to see the incongruities in situations, starts with thinking. When you **think** fun, you start making fun. You become active and develop skills that produce fun in everyday experiences.

Passive fun, allowing a person or thing to give you enjoyment, can bring immediate gratification but with a price tag. It doesn't take a lot of effort to reach for alcohol, marijuana, pills, or fattening foods to give us a feeling that we're having fun. **Substance-abuse** is the most popular inefficient pathway to "fun" because it is so easy, immediate, and produces a powerful "fun" feeling. If a person has difficulty developing approaching skills, if he is lonely, often booze or pot can do the trick of allowing him to feel better without any of the skills required to meet the needs of belonging or worth. Substance-abusing is popular because it works. It is the most efficient of the inefficient pathway of "meeting" all eight needs. The substance-abuser feels in-control over his needs, even though the opposite is true. No new skills or people are required in taking a drink or downing a pill, yet the need for pleasure is met because the person doing the abusing feels good in a very short period of time. All substance-abusing dulls the mind's capacity to compare perceptual differences. Closing the differences between what we need and what we have brings a feeling of comfort to the person who is force-feeding or chain-smoking. But, check those prices! When the substance wears off, the person is left with the same lack of skills **plus remorse**. Usually his health is compromised since all chemicals in the body affect the natural function of our organs and brain. If a person finds pleasure mainly through food, obesity results and his feelings of worth and faith in himself are quickly obscured each time he passes a mirror. Heavy smokers run a terribly high risk of cancer, heart disease, and certainly chronic obstructive pulmonary (lung) disease. Alcohol and drugs attack your liver, kidneys, and brain, at the very least. It seems crazily inefficient to me that so many people work hard all week simply to destroy themselves "having fun" on weekends.

A few years ago I saw a client who was destroying herself with substances. This thirty-eight year old woman was smoking and drinking, and by her own admission, paying serious negative prices. Her children, who were eleven and thirteen, were complaining all the time about "bad air," dirty ashtrays, and smelly furniture and clothes. Her boyfriend couldn't stand her cigarette breath, yellow fingers, and stale clothes. He also couldn't accept her drinking and becoming obnoxious in public. He gave her an ultimatum: "Stop smoking and drinking or I'll be history."

When I asked her what she wanted, she said she wanted to stop all vices. She knew nicotine and alcohol were harming her health. She knew her children were upset, and she was convinced that her boyfriend would leave. She also had known all of this for the last five years, yet she still chose to smoke and drink to excess.

I asked her, "What do you want from me?" She had plenty of motivation to quit, if she really wanted to.

She said, "I've been to other shrinks , medical doctors, a palm reader, and even a health farm to dry out, but nothing has worked to get me to change." She looked up at me and stopped talking as if to say, "Now it's your turn."

Since I was fresh out of magic, and I'm sure that's what she wanted, I began to teach her Skill Building and the rethinking process. I asked if there were anything else she wanted to change besides stopping smoking and drinking. She said she would like her children to stop complaining, her boyfriend to never leave her, and she would like to be eighteen again. I asked what did she really want, and she looked at me with a stunned expression as if I hadn't been listening. She repeated what she had just said and added, "To feel better and end these problems."

In her mind, her problems were the excessive smoking and drinking, which caused problems with her kids, boyfriend, and health. In my mind, **the drinking and the smoking were her choices for a solution to her problems**. Both made her feel good, except it was only temporary. The problem was she wasn't meeting her needs enough. She didn't have enough efficient skills to find alternative pathways for all her needs, especially fun, belonging, and worth. **That is always the real problem when you feel bad—not having enough efficient skills to meet your needs**.

She learned that everything we think and do is purposeful to meet our needs—that her smoking and drinking were purposeful for need fulfillment. After reviewing all eight needs, she decided she was especially getting fun while she smoked and drank. The alcohol was also giving her a little security and freedom since when she drank she didn't care about her problems. Was she losing any needs when she used these substances? Yes. She was losing belonging with her children and boyfriend, and she was losing health because her body was deteriorating. She also suffered a loss in self-worth since she didn't like herself when she abused. She lost faith by not really believing in her ability to change. She decided that the price was too heavy, and she would try anything for more happiness.

I asked if working to stop her habits had been successful. She answered, "Of course not!" I explained that since what she was doing was meeting some needs, and since her needs were not going to go away, unless she could learn new pathways to meet the needs that smoking and drinking were now meeting, no attempts at stopping would ever be successful.

The task was to ask her to make a value judgment that developing different pathways to put fun, security, and freedom into her life would reduce the desire to use substances. Then I would teach her the five areas of rethinking.

By our fifth session, we made an achievement plan to practice efficient skills to put fun in her life. (You will be reading about these shortly.) With new skills to meet her need for fun, her belonging and self-worth improved. As she developed even more skills by rethinking, she felt for the first time she had control to keep happiness in her life beyond the time when she was smoking or drinking.

Another inefficient pathway to produce fun is compulsive **gambling**. Compulsive gamblers are driven to play at any cost. Actually, those who select gambling and a compulsion to win as pathways, are rarely meeting their need for fun. Usually they are trying to meet their need for worth through winning. No matter how much they win, it is never enough because in a short while, they will need more worth. Their aim is to compete against an unbeatable system and win despite the odds. There is a powerful sense of worth that comes from putting down five or ten dollars and hitting the twenty-to-one house odds. What other kind of investment returns a thousand percent profit like when you put a coin into a slot machine and win a jackpot? But for compulsive gamblers, no matter how many jackpots are won, they put the money back in, believing they can keep winning over and over. They really keep **losing** over and over, but their worth is tied to the anticipation of the next jackpot, that big win, and they just cannot stop. In all of the times I have visited Las Vegas, (which is not called "Lost Wages" for nothing), I have yet to see someone hit a jackpot and walk away with their winnings. Gamblers, like substance-abusers, need to find more efficient ways to meet their need for worth if they are ever going to stop gambling. The risks such people take cancel out the fun process they may experience from their activities. Some compulsive gamblers get mixed up with criminal elements involved in illegal gambling and take tremendous physical risks, as well as getting in way over their heads financially.

Similarly, people drive themselves to win against all odds, often risking their lives in ridiculous, **life-threatening contests** for worth—what a price! A few years ago Evel Knievel, despite preliminary trials indicating no man could leap over the Grand Canyon even with an atomic power-pack on a vehicle, insisted on making this daredevil stunt. He almost died. I wonder how much fun all those months in the hospital were for him!

Less dangerous, but equally inefficient pathways to meet the need for fun are, **waiting for others to entertain us, gossiping**, or **name-dropping**. These are all vicarious fun-making because each depends on others to provide the pleasure. These pathways may also provide a form of vicarious belonging and worth, so people continue to use them. Although inefficient, they do meet certain needs. Unfortunately, the vicarious thrill of feeling good by dropping names of important people in your life takes away from your feelings of worth for your own achievements. Gossiping may give a feeling of superiority over the person being talked about, but it costs belonging if it gets back to the other person or if the recipient of the gossip starts wondering if they're next. A gossip may soon find himself without anyone to talk to, or about!

There are many efficient pathways to bring fun and pleasure into your life. No one could possibly live long enough to explore the myriad of pathways to being a fun-maker and putting fun in his world. Yet many people find themselves in ruts. If that's the case for you, let me reacquaint you with ways to put fun into your life to become an efficient fun-maker.

First let me emphasize that everyone possesses skills to put fun into his life no matter how boring he believes himself to be. If you search inside yourself, you can remember many times in your life you had a laugh so hearty that your jaws and sides ached. Think back even into your childhood. Can you recall it? Tears streaming down your face and you're holding your stomach because it hurts from laughing so hard. Keep that feeling.

You can make that kind of fun happen regularly in all areas of your life. You really can. Not only can you, but if you want to be truly healthy, you must create fun, pleasure, and laughter. Laughter itself produces an important physiological function in the body. When you laugh, lungs are exercised, circulation improves, diaphragm extends, more oxygen gets to the blood, and your muscle tone improves. Laughter can alleviate pain—physical and emotional. Laughter helps people get through impossibly difficult situations. It keeps you young and prolongs life. Without a sense of humor, the value of life is diminished, and nothing seems to be worth much.

So let's get down to promoting a lifestyle which enables us to create fun in all our endeavors and to perceive the world as a humorous, fun-filled place. The first step involves perceptions of oneself. "Adults" may see themselves as "together," cool, reserved, and invisible. "Invisible is miserable." Remember? **The way to promote fun is to first evaluate you want more, and then rethink that it's okay to drop the serious act;** enjoyment depends on taking the risk of being seen and heard. It's awfully hard to hide a belly laugh.

There are many choices you control that create fun-making pathways, and most of them require only simple achievement plans that you can begin right away. One of the easiest popular fun-making activities is **trivia**. *Trivial Pursuit* has to be the hottest game of the mid-eighties, having made a fortune for its developers in a short time. Even though the pursuit of trivia seems adult enough, intellectual enough, it's the kind of action that not only gets you out of the rut of boredom, but brings people together, meeting several needs at once. The risk of acquiring trivia is zero, and since everyone has some sort of trivia in his head, it won't make us feel terribly different. Any bookstore has books on trivia. *The Book of Lists,* by Wallace et al, is one. It is fun just spending ten or fifteen minutes a day pursuing a new interest whether it's picking up a book before you go to sleep or while awaiting your morning coffee. Just think how much of a kick you'll get coming to work with a smile on your face, approaching a co-worker with a bit of trivia like, "Do you have any idea how many millionaires there are in America? Would you believe that in 1981 there were 580,384 millionaires?" Perhaps your boss might surprise you when you ask him if he knows which two companies produced the greatest number of millionaires in the country, and he answers, "McDonald's and Walt Disney Productions." Even so, you might come back at him with some **super** trivia like the information that Walt Disney and Ray Krock, founder of McDonald's, drove an ambulance together in 1917. At that time they were sixteen and seventeen, yet already talked about how they would have creative businesses when they owned their own companies. They had decided at that early time that they would allow their employees to share in the profits of the company, based on contribution to growth.

When you get involved in trivia, you'll find you will hold people's attention and involvement. Chances are, the person with whom you shared trivia will share with you in return. It's infectious. Tell the truth, when you read about the millionaires weren't you intrigued? Didn't it stir up some trivial information in you? So, trivia not only **gives** pleasure; it **gets** pleasure, knowledge, and belonging, in return.

Fun is part of every **sports** activity as long as you stay mostly in the process and don't lose the fun of playing by concentrating solely on the outcome. If you play to win (outcome) at any cost, you're sacrificing fun in an inefficient attempt at worth. The efficient pathway to have fun is to enjoy playing (process). If you play to win, and you do, you have fun and worth. When you lose, you have neither. When you play to build skills, you will have fun and worth regardless of whether you win or lose. I always ask myself, "Do I want to play for fun or worth or both?" That attitude has changed my life. Now, winning is only a bonus on top of already feeling good.

I also perceive Lifeskills sports in a different way from the kinds of sports that are limited to robust, very fit, young people. Schools still emphasize soccer, kickball, football, basketball, volleyball—fine activities, but only a select few excel in them, and they excel only for a brief period of their lives.

Lifeskills sports are those that one can participate in throughout life, and they are activities that one can enjoy without being exceptionally athletically endowed. I'm referring to sports like tennis, golf, jogging, swimming, biking, hiking, skiing, canoeing, skating, camping, aerobics, or many others that can be done from age five to one hundred and five, and in most cases without a lot of people. Lifeskills sports require little or no equipment and don't necessarily emphasize winning.

If you are rusty at sports, begin slowly—develop your strength and abilities as you go. Think of the sense of worth, faith, knowledge, and health you will be gaining along with the fun of doing it. It doesn't take much time or planning to begin to rethink and take action to have fun in a sport. You can even make an achievement plan to improve skills in a sport with which you are already familiar. What is important is that you are growing through doing.

Games are a great way to bring fun and belonging into your life. Indoor games are less physical than sports and rely more on intellect. You might have the urge to compete to win with indoor games too, but remember, the fun is really in playing and not necessarily winning. People who tantrum when they are losing a game or sport, choose angering to gain back the worth they fear they are losing. Of course, with angering they lose belonging and fun for sure!

If you want a shortcut that will help you avoid the competitive edge, you might consider "un-games" like putting together a thousand piece puzzle or doing a paint-by-numbers with someone. When you play table games, charades, *Trivial Pursuit,* or cards, you are choosing a vehicle that will bring people together. You have the ability to choose to have fun and achieve togetherness, no matter who wins.

The variety of games is so enormous, it's fun just browsing through a toy department or bookstore to select one or two. There are games of logic like chess or *Strategy,* games of luck like cards or dice, and word games like *Scrabble.* If you're a sports enthusiast, there are games designed to test your skills or knowledge. If you love mystery stories, there are games designed just for your tastes. The assortment is mind-boggling, from simple boardgames to electronic games that entertain you while you play. You can go from checkers to *Atari*. And, you have total control over which game you choose to play, who you play with, and what you choose to get out of the experience.

Leave games, and imagine yourself in the shower! Have you ever had a bad time singing in the shower? I hope you're not one who is so worried about being tone-deaf that you haven't indulged in that marvelous pleasure—letting go and singing at the top of your lungs! What a waste of pleasurable experience if you were so concerned with someone else's opinion that you didn't allow yourself to sing. Or dance. Or play music. Talk about fun, why, last week while driving to work, I sang along with Frank Sinatra. Frank and I sounded so good, I started planning our concert tour. Just then, pulling up to a red light, I noticed the family in the car to my left staring at me as though I were stark, raving mad. I smiled and waved. It can be very difficult being a singing star!

The point is, fun depends on the attitude you bring to it, and it means taking risks of not always acting like the super-cool adult others may expect you to be. Considering the enjoyment of making music, you may want to risk learning to play an instrument or burst into song in front of others. A wonderful idea would be to laminate song lyrics in plastic, so that I couldn't forget the words to some song the next time I am singing and scrubbing away in the shower. I remember visiting a friend several years ago. His father, was in the shower singing, ". . . and a million guitars, and a million guitars." He paused briefly, forgetting the words, then continued, "That's **two** million guitars!" The reverberating laughter started our day on a high note.

Consider the enjoyment you might derive from buying a songbook to learn some songs. Or, what about finally taking those guitar or piano lessons you've been putting off for ages? There's no time like the present to make an achievement plan to put more **music-making** in your life—it's a wonderful pathway to fun.

Dancing is making music with your body. It feels good, and it's good for you. If you haven't danced in a while, it may not feel comfortable going out on the dance floor pretending you are Fred Astaire. Still there are many resources to which you can turn. Television is a good source for learning about the latest dance craze. If that sort of dancing isn't for you, there are classes at the Y, local dance studios, or classes in aerobic jazz dancing, that don't require a partner. All this spells risk-taking, but you're not going to have fun or be a fun-maker by sticking to the sofa, vegetating, allowing your body to run down. Depressing is practically impossible out on the dance floor.

Recall the last time you watched someone do a **magic** trick. Were you bored, pained by it, feeling that your time was being wasted? I am confident that your full attention was on who-ever was doing the magic. Since childhood, I've been abso-lutely captivated by those marvelous people who could make things disappear, appear out of nowhere, and then make eve-rything vanish into thin air. I was always mesmerized, mysti-fied, and I still get a charge today watching a good magic trick being done. The difference is, today I participate—I'm no longer an observer. I used to think magic took some kind of very special talent until I started doing my own tricks. Magic books and tricks are available at many stores, even your own library. Sleight-of-hand is so easy! Anyone can do it, anyone willing to take a risk and grow! There are a number of tricks that look difficult and mystifying, but once you're in on the "secrets" they are very simple. People just love participating and trying to figure out the secret. Let me give you one party trick to illustrate how unmagical magic can be. This trick is called "Mind Reading."

The audience is introduced to a "mind reader." Our mind reader knows that when she leaves the room, the host (or other accomplice to the trick) will have the audience select an object somewhere in the room on which the group is to concentrate. When the mind reader returns, she will be asked a series of questions by the accomplice: "Is it Joe's book? Is it the American flag? Is it that pen on the table?" etcetera. The mind reader knows when the correct item is named, because the accomplice knows **when** to ask the right question. Just before the correct object is asked, the object questioned is something of the color black.

I guarantee that everyone will be involved, and the fun for all who participate in this magical trick will be enhanced. It doesn't take a lot of work or practice to do any of the simple tricks. Who knows, you may become the Houdini of your social group. At any rate, you'll have a lot of fun along the way, and you'll be bringing fun into the lives of others. Magic tricks make you a fun-maker.

Comedians are fun-makers. If you can tell a joke, you are a comedian. Like doing magic, **telling jokes** makes you visible and involves taking risks. Of course, a comedian needs to have jokes to tell. If you want to be a person with funny stories or jokes, you'll want to do some homework. You can write down funny things to say and then practice telling them. Scary stuff? It can be at first, especially if you mess up punchlines and get the timing all wrong. It may help to know that there are no born comedians. People are not born with jokes coming out of their mouths. Even Bob Hope, Joan Rivers, or Bill Cosby, learned jokes and how to deliver them. Comics learn to be good joke tellers just as plumbers learn how to fix leaky pipes. It takes information, having a joke file, and practice. Your first assignment, should you choose to accept it, is making a joke file.

I recently read a story about a fellow who works as a toll collector on the Eads Bridge which spans the Mississippi River between St. Louis and southern Illinois. He has spent thirty-three years collecting tolls on the same bridge but has only enjoyed the last four years. What changed?

Well, he started telling the corniest jokes he could find. Every morning he would tape a new joke to his tollbooth—but only the first half of the joke. Commuters would have the opportunity to supply the punchline. For example, one day he displayed, "What do Winnie the Pooh and Jack the Ripper have in common?" The answer, which he kept hidden, is: "The same middle name."

Of course, not all the people laugh or even participate. The jokes are dumb some of the time, but he is having fun at his job, feeling creative and worthy because it is a real achievement finding a new joke for each day. He is also experiencing more belonging than ever before. In fact, people have to be pushed along because they want to stop, chat, and give him their best jokes.

Because of the media, we can take advantage of good jokes at all times everywhere. There are jokes on the radio, television, tollbooths, in magazines, newspapers, tapes, records, lectures—even bathroom walls, if your taste happens to run to funny graffiti. There are nightclubs that specialize in joke-telling, comedy cabarets where new performers, along with. the seasoned comics, test out their material. To begin to develop your joke file, have a notebook with you so you can copy down what you hear. There isn't a single important comedian who doesn't have a joke file. This is one area where it's okay to steal; jokes are common domain, unless they aren't funny.

After you've accumulated some material, learn how to tell a joke. Get a tape recorder, so you can hear your own voice inflections and tone, and listen to how well you time the punchline. Watch yourself to see how funny your expressions are. Even though some comics get away with deadpan, most people respond best to someone whose face helps tell the story. After you have rehearsed one or two jokes, so that you are comfortable delivering them, test them out with a friend or relative. A little enthusiasm goes a long way and sometimes carries the joke for you. When you're ready and rarin' to go, remember there's a time and a place for everything. If your mother-in-law is talking about her day shopping, it wouldn't be appropriate to interrupt her by announcing you have a "knock-knock" joke you're just dying to tell. If you can manage to fit your joke material into the topic of conversation, the funnier it will seem. That means, the more comfortable you become with joke-telling and the more jokes you have to draw from, the better your success as a fun-maker will be. After all, if pygmy jokes are the only ones you know, it's questionable how many conversations you can naturally jump into. (Speaking of pygmies, do you know what you get when you cross a pygmy with a vampire? You get a short sucker about three feet tall!)

Once you get your joke file together, you can expand it to include miscellany designed to have fun and make fun. I have a fun file with years of accumulated goodies taken from magazines, books, movies, television, nightclubs, ideas from other people, or things I have thought up myself. My fun file not only contains jokes, it has puzzles, cartoons, games, interesting inexpensive places to visit, funny articles, silly photographs, restaurant information, even toys. The possibilities for your fun file are unlimited. Why wait until Aunt Matilda comes to town to discover the interesting and fun things to do around town? Wherever you live, I know there are interesting, fun places, ethnic neighborhoods with colorful activities, or stores that are neat to shop. Perhaps there are historical sites or natural wonders which you have put off visiting on your own. With a little bit of money, you and a friend could explore and determine which is the best inexpensive restaurant in town. Some imagination and effort could lead to exciting, fun-filled possibilities. Your fun file will give you knowledge, but only you can choose to use it. Remember, your choice for happiness starts with evaluating, and then rethinking to begin an action plan.

Earlier I asked you to think back into your childhood to remember the kind of fun that sent you into free, non-"adult," side-splitting laughter. Now I'm going to ask you to bring your uninhibited childhood into today. If you can't draw on the freeness of your own childhood fun-making, spend some time around little children and observe the fun they have. Notice how free and spontaneous they are, how easy it is for them to pretend and totally lose themselves in play. If you make a list of childlike behaviors, activities, games, interactions, you might begin to recall what it felt like as a child.

To get rid of the uptight actions of a "grown-up" and get back to **childlike freedom**, why not do what kids do? I believe that the more childlike you are, the less self-critical you are. How long has it been since you played tag or hopscotch or jump-rope? If it's been ten, twenty, or fifty years, you're in for a wonderful treat. It's not just a cliche that youth is wasted on the young—if you begin to play a childhood game with another adult, you'll discover that the fun may be better now than it was then.

A few years ago, Suzy and I decided to have a "Kid Party" for several of our adult friends. It began with everyone coming to the house dressed in old clothes and tennis shoes. None of the guests knew what we were going to do, but they agreed to go along and "play" the way they did as children. We played "Hide and Seek," "Simon Says," and "Red Rover."

There were side games of jacks, hopscotch, ropejumping, and "horse." Twenty adults, ranging in age from thirty to past fifty, running up and down my (otherwise very conservative) suburban neighborhood, created quite a picture! We played from four-thirty in the afternoon until nine at night, and by the time we had "hid and sought" ourselves punchy, filling the air with hilarity, half the neighbors had joined in. Most of the people on the block talk about it to this day. Everyone wonders when we're going to do it again.

You could hold your own kid party. Drawing from your list of childlike activities, you could play "Simon Says," "Musical Chairs," or "Kick-The-Can." You could build sand castles, have snowman parties or mud pie parties. You could have pillow, squirt gun, or water balloon fights. You could even make a bunch of whipped cream pies and choose up teams in the yard on a warm sunny day. A friend of mine did the unthinkable last summer: He invited twenty of his teenage son's friends and their fathers over for the afternoon. They played croquet, volleyball, softball, relay races, corn-husking contests, and ended with printed pages for a sing along. One father said, "I didn't know my son could sing so well," and a son said, "I never saw my Dad have so much fun before." I know you will feel like a new person by allowing yourself the risk of acting like a kid again.

Finally, as a Skill Builder you are responsible for **personal choices** regarding what feels pleasurable to you. Even if you don't have a great deal of money to spend on putting fun into your life, you still have infinite choices. Perhaps your pathway is collecting matchbook covers, or maybe painting is your thing. You might find that a sport is your pathway, or you could choose cooking. The activities should meet your needs. If your pathways are unique to you, they won't require anyone else's permission or approval. If you have loved snakes all your life, go for it, even if your mother swears she'll never set foot in your house. If you've been itching to learn to play the piano, do it.

If you have extra money to spend, you can find delicious fun-making activities to fill your life from flying airplanes to ski parties in Lucerne. You can satisfy your curiousity for far away places by traveling which creates fun in planning and shopping for the trip, as well as in taking it. You can invest in an elaborate hobby like stained glass, ceramics, or stamps. Perhaps your greatest pleasure would be restoring an antique car.

The idea of all these suggestions is that fun is a need which can be met in more ways than you have hairs. Whether at work, religious service, or in your own back yard, you can meet your need for fun. You don't need money or youth. All you need is the ability to observe, think, and realize that fun is everywhere for the person who risks reaching for it.

I'm not sure if all the world loves a lover. But I am sure that it loves a **laugher**, especially if he is a **laughmaker**. You'll find that efficient pathways to put fun in your life meet all of your other needs. When all your needs are met, the stress in your life is reduced. Who wouldn't want to live a life that makes the world a fun place to be? From WHMPA-Land to the world of Skill Building is only a laugh apart.

CHAPTER THIRTEEN

KNOWLEDGE

"I am too old to learn."

WhMPA

"All our knowledge has its origins
in our perceptions."

Leonardo da Vinci

KNOWLEDGE

Do you picture yourself an interesting person?

Do you see special things about each person you talk to?

Do you watch one program on educational television each week?

Do you ask open-ended questions?

Do you read about topics you know nothing about?

Do you cram for tests?

Do you or did you cheat when taking a test?

Do you try new things even if they might not be fun?

Do you brainstorm positive choices to solve problems?

Are you self-critical?

Do you picture yourself doing a task successfully before you start it?

Does your mind wander when you are listening to others?

Do you teach others to memorize new information?

Do you look in the dictionary to learn new words?

Each time something negative occurs, do you purposefully take time to learn something from the situation?

While driving, do you listen to talk shows on the radio?

Do you read parts of the newspaper each day?

Do you take time each day to focus on one of your five senses?

Do you exchange ideas with others each day?

"You can't teach an old dog new tricks," is a cliche that is not true. Improvement is not a trick, and we are not dogs. As humans, we have a need for knowledge to enable us to gain more happiness. If we can develop efficient skills in **sensing**, **creating**, and **thinking** we will achieve more of what we need.

I recall how I hated Sunday nights when I was a student, forcing down pages and pages of facts in order to pass a test the next day or to be able to answer questions in class. These Sunday night cramming sessions were hardly meeting my need for knowledge, since by Tuesday I'd forget most of the facts I had so quickly squeezed into my head. I was working only to pass the exam, look good in class, and enhance my self-worth. I was not working to learn new information.

Genuine knowledge means having skills to learn and deal with what life brings. I am sure you have heard the saying, "Knowledge is power." This is not entirely true. Knowledge is power **only if** you use it efficiently and work to expand on rethinking the five areas of: out-of-control to in-control, want to need, forced to choice, outcome to process, and negative stress to positive stress. The more you use rethinking, instead of reacting, the more power you will have. Power is not knowing how to change others to get your needs met, but in knowing how to change yourself to feel better.

Life is an ongoing process of input. Therefore, everyone has the opportunity to learn. The avenues for learning have never been better than right now. As John Naisbett, author of *Megatrends*, tells us, "We are drowning in information data and starving for knowledge." Did you know that from 1750 to 1900 information in the world doubled? From 1980 to 1983 it doubled again! As the time periods have shortened, the amount of material has increased almost beyond control. We all know we can't digest everything, yet some of us will take in more than others. Why? Motivation is one reason; having learning skills is another.

A truly bright, creative person, responds to the stimuli around her. She is extremely alert to sounds and changes in tones and is aware of distracting noises. A bright person is tactilely aware of a firm handshake, how textures feel, how clothes fit. Brightness skills begin with **sensing** the little details many of us miss.

Bright people sit in the front of the classroom and listen instead of daydreaming. They wear a "different set of lenses," a much sharper set, when they sense the world. Comedians with staying power such as George Carlin, Joan Rivers, Jonathan Winters, Gallagher, and Robin Williams sense a "normal" situation differently. They have trained themselves to see details, causes, strangeness in many daily activities that pass most of us by. With sensing skills they will always have the capacity to take in more and help us see the fun in our world.

Unfortunately, most people take their senses for granted. If you wish to gain more knowledge, which means more alternatives, become aware of how sensing is the gateway to growth. Thinking too much can actually reduce the information our senses are picking up. Picture the last time you were in a group being introduced to several new people. Did you have trouble remembering their names? Were you the one who said, "I can always remember faces, but I just can't keep names in my head"? If this happens often, it may be because you are so busy **thinking** of the name or worried about what you are going to say in response. When we are overly concerned with making our response, the only name we remember from an introduction is our own. By thinking, you negated the sensory input of the person you were meeting. You won't be able to sense input and therefore learn if you are thinking about something or someone else. In other words, you can't be internal and external at the same time! Next time you're meeting a new group of people, to remember a person's name I suggest you stop long enough to pick up sensory cues. Shake his hand and identify his touch. Look into his eyes and put a picture of him in your mind, while allowing yourself to hear the tone of his voice. An introduction which involves most of your senses will be a lasting impression.

To be bright you must first become a good sensor. You might feel what I am going to suggest is silly or inconsequential. But if you want to build muscles, isn't it necessary to practice using them? If you want to learn more information, you can choose to increase your sensing skills by practicing the following exercises. Begin by finding out what the thresholds of your senses are. Ask yourself where your blindspot is—how extensive is your field of vision? Whether at home, the office, or a familiar restaurant, it is predictable that you have looked repeatedly at your environment without seeing the details. Get in touch with what you see, with how far your peripheral vision extends, with what kinds of light please you, and which colors you cancel out.

Next, concentrate on your hearing. Can you hear sound beyond the room you're in? Can you pick up a faraway siren or a car alarm on the street? If it's summer, can you hear the crickets outside or the birds? By becoming aware of sounds, you can expand the things your ears pick up, adding to your knowledge about what is going on around you, both near and far.

Touch includes more than what your fingers sense. Close your eyes and try to become aware of how your toes feel against the tops and bottoms of your shoes. Move to your waist and concentrate on the skin under your waistband or belt. Does your mid-section tell you something about your weight? How does the skin on your back and shoulders respond to the material of the shirt or blouse you are wearing? You can carry out this exercise on all parts of your body, identifying the sensations each inch of you feels.

What kind of taste is in your mouth? Can you still sense the flavors of the pepperoni pizza you had for lunch, or is your mouth filled with the flavor of chewing gum? Is the taste dry or wet? Are your teeth clean or fuzzy? Explore the tastes and sensations inside your mouth, moving outward to the sense of smell.

What odor can you pick up from the room you're in? Dust or cooking odors left from last night? Or does the open window carry the scent of freshly cut grass into the room? How far does your sense of smell reach? Are you conscious of the smell of your own soap, the scent from your cologne, the lingering traces of your shampoo? Can you tell where the bakery is when you drive through a strange town? Does you sensor fire off when you pass McDonald's?

Becoming a sensor means you are changing what you are taking in from the world. You are rethinking and then interpreting your perceptions differently. To become a good sensor, you can make a plan. Allow yourself five minutes a day to attend to your senses and how well they pick up what is going on around you. Make a checklist of what you sense that is new, interesting, or previously overlooked. It will keep you focused on this rethinking process of sensing. Sensing more of your world takes practice, but soon you will go beyond using just one or two senses when you meet someone.

When you become a multiple sensor, you will find you have complete control over gathering better quality information which will stay with you longer. When all your senses are developed and you are consciously reacting to them, you will achieve greater need fulfillment, especially in belonging and fun. An exercise to help you practice being a multiple sensor is one in which, fully conscious of using all your senses, you approach a familiar person. Notice how his hair gives off a scent you might have overlooked. Become conscious of his shiny skin; hear an accent you hadn't heard before.

Choose to tell the first friend you see tomorrow morning one specific thing you like about the way he looks, smells, or sounds. You can always shake hands for a socially acceptable touch. You can also practice walking down your street, opening your senses to sights, sounds, and smells you have taken for granted until now. You may be amazed how much you've missed. By the way, do you know the names of the streets around you for a mile in every direction?

Another pathway for more efficient sensing is to rethink using the word **what** instead of **why**. When you ask a question which begins with "Why," you involve the intellect (internal) instead of the senses (external). When a question begins with "What," its answer is a descriptive one requiring the use of your senses. "Why" questions are usually followed by "Because" answers which can lead to over-intellectualizing. "Why are you doing this?" "Because this is what I want to do," can go on forever in a series of more and more "Why"s, until one gets trapped into nothing but asking, "Why?" There may be hundreds of valid, accurate answers to "Why" questions. However, when you ask, "What are you doing?" "I'm enjoying a book called *Happiness, It's Your Choice,*" you're into description. You are specific and definite about what you are doing, and you are taking actions to move forward. You aren't offering excuses for doing what you're doing, and you won't frustrate yourself with thinking in circles.

When you rethink to have only "What" questions in your head, you will want to have descriptive words to answer those questions. If your words are not as descriptive and specific as you would like, you have an excellent opportunity to expand your vocabulary. I rely on my thesaurus, keeping one at my home and one at my office, so that I have access to new words at all times. As a specific sensor, you will not be satisfied with generalized words like **nice, good, fine**, etcetera. Rather than writing, "Burt sure is a nice guy," you will need words to describe Burt's crystal blue eyes, rugged good looks, or the musky scent of his hair. Instead of noting that your plane trip was "just fine," you will want to describe the soothing effects of the color scheme, the comfortable rhythm of the engine, and the smoothness of the flight. In addition to a thesaurus, consider the new desk calendars which provide a new word every day or putting your own new word up on your mirror every evening, making it an achievement plan to use that new word at least three times during the next twenty-four hours. You might make a plan to use a word game regularly to practice vocabulary building.

I recall how in high school I wanted an extensive vocabulary, so people would think I was intelligent. I was envious of students who did well—something I now know I had no control over. One particular friend, Mack, was bright, a good athlete, and a real achiever. He was knowledgable about other things beyond academics, sports, politics, and social gossip. All this information made Mack a very popular person, especially since he was positive and usually willing to help others with their problems. I wanted to be popular in school like Mack. I wanted to achieve in academics and participate in athletics and extracurricular activities. I wanted to do it all and be the best. But no matter how hard I studied, Mack always did a little better. Not only that, he seemed to always know a little more about everything! I was frustrated and couldn't figure out what to do because I wanted to be like Mack. I knew if I quit sports, clubs, and dating, to study more, I'd be even more unhappy. There just weren't enough hours in the day to work to be better than Mack.

After I started graduate school at Washington State University, I learned what Mack had been doing differently. I took a class in sensation and perception, started applying what I was learning, and changed my life. It had taken me almost ten years to learn Mack's secret.

When I recall my high school days, Mack was always "there" in each class, never goofing off, really listening, asking questions, sitting up front, sensing what the teacher was saying. What was I doing in class? Frequently, I was thinking about after-school time sports, the dance on Friday, and daydreams that took me away. I believed I could get away with daydreaming because I could study at night or over the weekends. I didn't realize that I was developing inefficient habits that made it hard for me to sense those boring text books in my filled-with-distractions home environment. Have you ever read five pages of a text, closed the book, and had no idea what you just read? That was me at home. I was not listening to me read. Most of the time I was still thinking about "whatever" while reading. Sensing is not just reading the pages or writing the assignment. It is choosing to see, hear, and when appropriate, use all your senses to take in information, as Mack was able to do so skillfully. Since I have learned to be a sensor, I never turn a page of text until I've asked myself, "What did I hear on that page?" When I can teach myself something new, I turn the page.

Next time you read an article in a magazine or newspaper, even if you are reading just for pleasure, try not turning the page until you ask, "What did I hear on that page?" Don't just wait for "important sources" of information to practice being a better sensor.

Another way to efficiently meet your need for knowledge is by extending your **creative skills**. Everyone in the world has creative thoughts, but they are not always positive. I've seen some very creative slightly crazy people in my time. WhMPAs discount or discard the creative thoughts that run through their minds, while inventors and artists act on them. It is unfortunate that creativity is discouraged by many schools and businesses, that the natural expansion of minds is inhibited by rules and rule-makers.

The more creativity you have, the more alternatives you can have to meet your needs. You can restore this facility by tuning in to your creative thoughts and letting them run free.

To enhance your own creativity, you must develop creative skills. The most important aspect of allowing the creative juices to flow is **forgetting outcome** and **thinking "process"**. With outcome in your mind, you restrict yourself from ideas that might be too risky to actually be put to use. It's okay to allow such ideas to flow. In fact, fantastic, impractical ideas may be your first step. So let the ideas come. Free-associate.

In rethinking, give up self-critical thoughts—they interfere with the process of creative thinking. In fact, fear of criticism, either others' or one's own, is the number one inhibitor of creative thoughts. Can you imagine what might have happened had Wilbur and Orville Wright been stopped with a thought like, "A machine that flies??? You must be kidding! No machine can defy gravity!" Or, if Al Jolson had scoffed, "Talking pictures?? What kind of funny cigarettes have you been smoking?"

All creative ideas and inventions start simply, although by the time they are perfected they may be quite complex. Creativity usually begins with a single step, a single idea that blossoms into larger steps and larger ideas. The inventors of the first airplane didn't consider the elaborate technologies that eventually led to the SST—they began at the beginning. When motion pictures were invented, sound synchronization, color, or special effects, were not part of the consideration—the focus was on making pictures on a screen. Believe me, if I had thought about writing every page and chapter to get this book published, I may never have begun the first sentence! So, in allowing your thoughts to spin creatively, remember that you are beginning a process that begins simply. Sometimes the first step for acting creatively comes from dreaming. You can do many creative things in your dreams which will prepare you for the next day.

Successful people learn the value of free-association in personal growth and in allowing ideas to expand and grow. In business, creative free-association is usually called "brainstorming." On occasion, I have observed a business person who has a creative thought and won't let go of it, even when others reject it. He lacks the faith that new creative thoughts will come to replace the one he is struggling to maintain. There are also men like Walt Disney, who had so many creative ideas, he never feared letting go of one because new creative thoughts were constantly replacing old ones. Disney trained his staff to brainstorm, so that everyone had the opportunity to contribute without criticism. He used to joke about never having "business" meetings. Disney felt that meetings were for critics to bring up reasons why things won't work. Instead, he promoted brainstorming what it takes to make ideas happen.

At the Center for Skill Development, we have our own "Walt Disney" in Pat Goehe. Pat is always thinking about what can be done, not why it won't work. Hopefully, you are fortunate enough to have a brainstormer at your job or home. If not, you could start to be the model.

To develop the skill of brainstorming, find a quiet, comfortable place. Begin by looking at some particular aspect of your world with which you are fairly familiar, like baseball, the weather, your role as a parent. Then ask yourself, "What if . . .?" This exercise is to begin to challenge familiar assumptions about an area with which you've become too familiar. No matter how silly it may seem, ask yourself, "What if . . .?" and don't put any limits on the shape the questions take. For example, you might ask yourself, "What if baseball catchers were midgets? Then they wouldn't have to squat." Have fun while you are being creative!

From "What if . . .?" questions, progress to looking at the similarities and differences between things you've gotten used to without contemplation. Try reversing all familiar notions about people, places, or things, and look at them as if you'd never seen them before. Or, reverse something strange to something you've known your entire life and with which you feel comfortable. You're stretching the limits of your conventional thinking by making the familiar strange and the strange familiar.

After completing and practicing these rethinking and brainstorming exercises, it's important to try your thoughts on another person. My good friend, Paul, and I used to play a brainstorming game called, "The Million Dollar Idea" every week. Our inventions included a pocket breath indicator, so people with bad breath wouldn't be the last ones to know, and a camp for adults, in southern California which was open every weekend all year 'round. You can choose to have regular brainstorming sessions with your family, but no objections are allowed. Each person may come up with ideas on any subject and about any family situation, no matter how far-out the idea may be. A brainstorming night might be a wonderful creative practice for everyone, and it could meet many other needs at the same time.

After practicing these new sensory and creative skills, I suggest you develop skills **to think** and evaluate more efficiently. The first step to more efficient thinking is to break down your new sensory or creative information into the smallest components possible. Grandiosity and fantasy-thinking may fulfill your needs, but they are not efficient ways of thinking. If you want to learn new material, the most efficient method is to feed that information to your brain in small steps. For example, I love golf and I am working at becoming a better golfer. I watch someone who is a very good golfer, and then I try to break down what he does in small, workable units I can follow. I use all of my senses in watching this professional, so I can take in as much knowledge as possible, and then I try to write an achievement plan using his performance as a model. I try to stay in the process. I don't think that I must hit a golf ball two hundred and eighty yards like Jack Nicklaus. Instead I think one key thought like putting my left shoulder under my chin so I can get a full shoulder turn on my backswing.

The second step to thinking more efficiently is visualizing. The object of visualization is to picture yourself doing a task successfully. You may have seen Dwight Stones, the American high jumper at the 1984 Olympics, using visualization. He was concentrating on his best possible form, going over and over again in his mind the action necessary to clear incredible heights. You could even see his head bob as he took imaginary steps, and then jump to clear the bar.

When you visualize yourself successfully carrying out an action, chances are you will not only be able to take that action, but will carry it out more easily. But, "over analysis can cause paralysis," so be careful not to overthink. By visualizing successive stages, you are building an efficient thinking skill that will give you an alternative to generalizing, intellectualizing, or self-critical, growth-inhibiting thoughts. Even if you make mistakes, the positive picture in your head will allow you to pick yourself up and try again because you have already visualized yourself successfully doing the action.

The most significant aspect of all of these exercises is that they are skill building. They start by evaluating what is working and then move into rethinking. Having efficient pathways to put knowledge into your life requires allowing yourself options. Spontaneity is a large part of what all new thinking is about whether it is creative or not. Rigidity prevents new information and new possibilities from entering our minds. If you are not controlling for outcome, your senses can bring you knowledge and new perceptions in every aspect of your life. Each day you could choose to learn something new and in so doing you will never be the same again.

CHAPTER FOURTEEN

HEALTH

"You make me sick."

WhMPA

"Stress does not have to be negative in context—even celebrating
Christmas can disrupt the
balance."

Paul Brenner, M.D.

HEALTH

Do you plan social gatherings that do not include eating or drinking?

Do you work to meet all your needs in all your environments?

Do you pay attention to the relationship between what you are doing and how you are feeling physically?

Do you practice moderation in food and drink?

Do you practice humor when you feel stressed?

Do you depend on others to keep you healthy?

Do you release your fork between bites?

Do you tell others your plan when you are working to change an inefficient habit?

Do you smoke cigarettes?

Do you follow an exercise plan for each day or each week?

Do you know the nutritive value of foods you eat?

Do you know and continue to learn about how specific parts of your body function?

Do you take walks every day?

Do you diet for weight loss?

Do you use salt from a salt shaker on your food?

Do you wait until you are hungry to consume a meal?

Do you choose friends who are concerned with their physical health?

Do you do your food shopping when you are not hungry?

Health is being in balance. If you are familiar with the holistic health movement, you have an understanding of what I mean by this statement.

When we meet all eight needs efficiently in all our environments, we will be happy and healthy. However, we have no control over what the environment gives us, and since we are not perfect, even the strongest Skill Builder will not efficiently meet all his needs all the time. This reality puts our health in a constant state of flux.

Whenever we experience the feeling of poor health, most of us perceive the bad feelings as negative signs. A Skill Builder knows that the signals of ill health are a friend just as stress is a friend. The symptoms of a cold, headache, high blood pressure, or any of the many physiological ailments that can plague us, are telling us something. The message is that we are either perceiving or doing something wrong. We are out of balance. Certainly we might call the family doctor for some advice or medication, but at the same time we could check out the need areas for any inefficiencies. Remember, all eight needs are equally important; there is no "one" need that is genetically more powerful. But because our needs are not always met with the same efficiency, we perceive those lacking fulfillment as very important. We can be achieving at work to feel worth, but be lonely if we are moving away from others. Without rethinking and acting to put our systems back in balance, poor health can occur.

Think of times in your life when the stress of not having one or more of your needs met resulted in an illness. I strongly suspect there are more cases of flu, colds, and stomach disorders around mid-April than there are in February and May. Staying up all hours of the night, overeating, undereating, or drugging seem to be rituals for many Americans during income tax time. If you are affiliated with a university, whether student or professor, can you identify with the end of the term panic over finals? The business community has inventory and fiscal year reports. We all have holidays and family crises which can upset the balance.

A WhMPA will often perceive the symptoms of poor health as a signal to change, but his pathways to put better health into his life are often inefficient. Remember, stress leads to motivation, but motivation doesn't tell you how to change efficiently. When stress breaks down his body, many times the WhMPA looks for **extreme solutions**. "Solutions" like withdrawing from a stressful job and choosing to stay on unemployment, or because of a rejection, choosing to isolate himself at home, or the extreme of tenacity—working harder and longer to attempt to change a bureaucracy to meet his needs.

The WhMPA may also look for **instant solutions**. Instead of making a plan to rethink and gradually change his lifestyle to a healthier one, a WhMPA may dash out to become an overnight jogger, weight-lifter, or health advocate, putting more strain and stress on his unfit body than if he had done nothing. If overweight, he might opt for a fad or crash diet. Diet books have topped the bestseller lists for years, and they will probably continue to do so because people are looking for the "miracle" diet to make them thin without effort on their part. All you have to do is pick up a *National Enquirer* or some other magazine (my favorite's the *Star*) and read about the "new diet" which "melts" pounds away—some even as you sleep! Even when some of the diets prove fatal, people continue choosing them jeopardizing their health to lose weight fast. A biology professor I knew suggested his version of a "while you sleep" diet. During the winter, sleep completely uncovered. His rationale was that your metabolism had to increase to maintain sufficient body heat to keep you alive. (This is assuming you have not compensated by increasing the thermostat!) Of course, not many people go for his diet. They not only don't want to make any effort, they don't want to be uncomfortable either!

The reality of dieting is that it's a **STOP** plan. You are working to stop eating those pleasurable foods that gratify your needs, especially for fun. I've never met a person who overdosed on celery, spinach, or cauliflower. It's cake, pie, cookies, ice cream, and the rest of that bunch that give us so much troublesome pleasure. When you diet and don't develop alternative pathways for fun and pleasure, you're acting inefficiently. Your need for fun is not going to go away, and therefore, dieting won't work.

Proper eating, combined with regular exercise and numerous alternatives to put pleasure and fun in your life when you are stressed or bored, will lead to a healthy body. Remember—achieving, moving toward others, learning a new task, exercising, or any other actions that meet any need will give you pleasure. So start rethinking to change your lifestyle, not just what you eat.

I know that developing alternative pathways for pleasure in lieu of dieting will work for lasting change. I know because I was a fat child who loved to sit and watch television and eat chocolate chip ice cream. When I was fifteen my mother took me to a doctor who helped me attain the kind of balance which has allowed me to stay at 165 (plus or minus five pounds) all my adult life. This doctor taught me a **START** program. I no longer thought of dieting as **stop**ing anything. Most of the time my thinking was focused on starting to look the way I wanted to look, starting to learn tennis and golf and other sports, or starting to become attractive to girls and to develop social skills. I was actually starting to be a fun maker with skills to rethink for the kind of acting that could permanently change my life.

It's amazing to me how many gullible people buy the fad health products that swamp the market these days. It is a very inefficient way to bring more health into your life and another one of those "instant" remedies for whatever ails you. Do you suffer from baldness? Then Genie Joe has the surefire tonic to miraculously make hair grow on a billiard ball! Is your chest too flat? Then you can buy the Boom-Boom Bosom Buster and become a full-busted woman within two weeks! The ads boast, "Your friends will never recognize you!" and "Take away your best friend's lover!" How about aging skin or sagging muscles? Surely you've heard that seventy year olds are regaining the youthful fresh looks of their twenties (or somebody else's, if their twenties weren't so hot) with Goniff's Glandular Extract. And, "Only $99.95 per half-ounce jar!" Millions of people seeking miracle cures keep these snake oil companies in business. I believe that most of the people who buy these "cures" are watching a lot of television where they see a succession of catastrophic problems resolved in thirty to sixty minutes. This gives an illusion that life's problems have quick solutions, and once you believe in "out there," commercials and advertisements present a pathway to get what you instantly want.

Another inefficient choice for health is **to become dependent on someone else for your well-being**. Being dependent on someone else to put your blood pressure pills in front of you, to remind you that you shouldn't use salt, or to ask you to stop after two sets of singles is not taking control over your own life. You might make the excuse that you're just too busy with work or obligations to be aware of those things, but balance in your life means taking control over the pathways to meet all your needs. Looking to others keeps you from being aware of your own body and your own responsibilites. One cannot experience the feeling of achievement in taking care of himself if he gives his spouse or secretary the job of reminding him whenever he needs to take his meds or watch his weight. And achievement is a pathway to meeting your need for worth.

Hypochondriacs often engage in dependent relationships where the partner is responsible for being the caretaker of their needs for security, worth, belonging, health, and even fun. They often get pleasure and enjoyment over fanatic details about their health, trying to control others into joining them and taking care of their needs, similar to the depressing person. The negative prices paid for these unbalanced relationships are high, causing both partners to feel better momentarily, but eventually making both weaker and feeling bad about the lifestyle in which they have "trapped" themselves.

The physiological and psychological prices paid for other inefficient pathways to meet your needs should be evaluated daily. You know yourself better than anyone else. You're the only one who can examine the unhealthful ways you are using to meet some of your needs right now. Are you on the "Valium" diet?—You lose weight because you are so relaxed that food falls off your fork, and you don't even care! Are your wants for worth being met by the kind of angering or powering that will result in getting your face punched in? Do you take pain reducers when you could find alternate pathways for pleasure or belonging? If your health is being endangered by meeting your needs in inefficient ways, it's time to rethink, to make healthier choices to meet your needs in a way that is positive for your entire well-being.

You can begin by making a plan to discover the pathways you control to meet your health each day in all of your environments. Consider what you are putting into your body for nourishment and in what amounts. Consider how active you are, and evaluate what you can do to improve your exercise regimen or cut it down if your weekend days are overactive. Think what you might do to bring balance into your thinking. What can you do when you are stressed to learn not to fear it in the future? What can you do to enhance your creativity each day? Think about the risks you can take to bring more belonging into your life; the phone call you might make to give someone enjoyment. One powerful skill to improve your health and to keep you healthy is laughter. As I noted in the chapter on Fun, humor and laughter are necessary ingredients for health, stimulating all the vital organs. In *Anatomy of an Illness,* Norman Cousins developed a program for health in the face of a life-threatening illness. His program helped him to regain his health and impressed me with his Skill Building approach. Here are Norman Cousins' six steps to health:

1. Realize that every human being has a built-in capacity for recuperation and repair.

2. Recognize that the quality of life is important.

3. Assume responsibility for the quality of your own life.

4. Nurture the regenerative and restorative forces within you.

5. Utilize laughter to create a mood in which the other positive emotions can be put to work for yourself and those around you.

6. Develop confidence and the ability to feel love, hope, and faith, and acquire a strong will to live.

During Cousins' battle with his painful and frightening illness, he watched Marx Brothers films, "Candid Camera" reruns, and devoured numerous books on humor. He wrote that one ten minute interlude of laughter generated two hours of restful sleep. The result of his pathway into humor was a reduction of the inflammatory disease that was killing him.

Test his theory out. Find some friends and play indoor games or have a tickling bout. Note what the laughter does to your body and your feelings. No matter what kind of pain you may be suffering—physical or psychological—it's doubtful you'll feel it while tears of laughter are streaming down your face. Lawrence Peter and Bill Dana, in *The Laughter Prescription,* theorize that laughter controls pain in four significant ways:

1. By changing attention
2. By reducing tension
3. By a change of attitude
4. By increasing the body's natural painkillers

They point out that pain intensifies if our minds focus on what is ailing us. There is relief by drawing attention away from what hurts. Tension can create pain—try tensing your eyebrows for a minute to test this out. Can you hold that tension for a full minute without it hurting? When we laugh, our muscles relax. It interested me to discover that the director of UCLA's Pain Control Unit, Dr. David Bressler, has made a correlation between chronic pain and chronic depression. Dr. Bressler said, "Almost always, people who have chronic pain are also depressed. It is not just their lower back which hurts; their life hurts. They have placed that hurt in their lower back." Laughter and humor not only amplify the will to live and reduce pain, they actually promote the body's endorphins (natural pain killers), speeding up the healing process. In addition, laughter seems to stimulate the brain to release a number of hormones including echolamine, a complex chemical consisting of epinephrine and norepinephrine, and dopamine, the response and alertness connection. Without laughter, it is doubtful a person can have a healthful existence. In trying to regain balance in any need area, you may have to overcompensate initially. The key word here is "initially." There is a difference between the compulsive fanatic and someone who temporarily overcompensates. If your life is nearly devoid of entertainment because you have been so involved with work, knowledge, or health, then you may need to pursue fun activities to the limit in order to get back into the habit of making fun a regular part of a balanced life. If you've neglected exercise too long, you may have to force yourself to push for an hour or so each day, not necessarily rigorously. For example, you might start out with a long walk in the morning and another at night. Eventually you will achieve balance and can work out regularly for twenty minutes a day.

You may also have several skills you haven't used for a long time but which you can choose to renew. Perhaps you were terrific at seeing the positive, having an optimistic attitude, but you're getting pessimistic about things. It's time to get back on track! Perhaps you brainstormed but have gotten bogged down in everyday activities. Now is the time to learn how to free-associate again and let the creative juices flow. If you're rusty at a sport, make the time to take it up again.

Another efficient pathway for increasing your health is to **learn how your body works**. Make this fun by accumulating health information as you would trivia. Then spring some health facts on everyone at the dinner table or at work. Presto! You have created a pathway for belonging and worth. For example, do you know how many bones there are in the human body? Two hundred and six. How about skin? Do you know how much there is on the average human body? Thirty-five hundred square inches. How many teeth does an adult have? Thirty-two. It is a fascinating fact though somewhat depressing, that only four percent of middle-aged people are physically fit! You might be surprised that it takes fifty muscles to frown but only thirteen to smile. Talk about inefficient and efficient actions! There are many resources for discovering facts and information about the human body from medical encyclopedias to health courses given by the Y or your local adult school. Would it be a different and entertaining way to start the day if you came to work and asked your boss if he knew what the human body is worth for its chemical make-up? Although we were only worth ninety-eight cents in the Forties, inflation has made us worth nearly six dollars today!

Developing a physical fitness program which meets more than one need is not only efficient, it helps keep us doing it! By joining an aerobics class rather than jumping up and down in your living room for a half hour alone each day, you'll be meeting your needs for belonging. You'll be having fun, and you'll also be doing a healthful activity. If you run or jog with a friend or a group, chances are you'll keep this a regular part of your daily program than if you run alone on dark streets where your only company is stray dogs. What if you look terrible in leotard and sweats? Really terrible? If you make stress your friend, you can find ways to use this as a means to meet other needs. How about working on your sense of humor? Try showing that you are capable of laughing at yourself by creating little jokes about those bulges. Develop your creativity by designing an original outfit which conceals them for the time being anyway! Start the process for belonging by "confessing" your uncomfortableness. You probably will discover your friends feel the same way!

Maintaining balance through laughter, knowledge, and physical fitness are some of the pathways that are necessary for a long healthy life. Since longevity is increasing, we can benefit from a life of Skill Building to successfully cope with the new stresses that longevity brings. Medical advances and better health practices mean that there are more elderly people today than at any time in history, and the numbers will be growing with each generation. The life expectancy for an American who is now thirty years old is seventy-seven or more—the highest life expectancy in the world. In order to adapt, a person needs information on what is or what will be. Following is a short quiz on the "Facts of Aging" taken from *The Gerontologist*. Let's see how much you already know!

T F   1. The majority of old people (past age 65) are senile—defective memory, disoriented, or demented.

T F   2. All five senses tend to decline in old age.

T F   3. Most old people have no interest in, or capacity for, sexual relations.

T F   4. Lung capacity tends to decline in old age.

T F 5. The majority of old people feel miserable most of the time.

T F 6. Physical strength tends to decline in old age.

T F 7. At least one-tenth of the aged are living in long-stay institutions—nursing homes, mental hospitals, homes for the aged.

T F 8. Aged drivers have fewer accidents per person than drivers under age 30.

T F 9. Most older workers cannot work as effectively as younger workers.

T F 10. About 80% of the aged are healthy enough to carry out their normal activities.

T F 11. Most old people are set in their ways, and unable to change.

T F 12. Old people usually take longer to learn something new.

T F 13. It is almost impossible for most old people to learn new things.

T F 14. The reaction time of most old people tends to be slower than reaction time of younger people.

T F 15. In general, most old people are pretty much alike.

T F 16. The majority of old people are seldom bored.

T F 17. The majority of old people are socially isolated and lonely.

T F 18. Older workers have fewer accidents than younger workers.

T F 19. Over 15% of the U.S. population is now age 65 or over.

T F 20. Most medical practioners tend to give low priority to the aged.

T F 21. The majority of older people have incomes below the poverty level, as defined by the Federal Government.

T F 22. The majority of old people are working or would like to have some kind of work to do, including housework and volunteer work.

T F 23. People tend to become more religious as they age.

T F 24. The majority of old people are seldom irritated or angry.

T F 25. The health and socioeconomic status of older people (compared to younger people) in the year 2000 will probably be about the same as now.

This test has been widely circulated with interesting results. Definite biases and misconceptions about the aging process occur regularly. The key to the correct answers is simple: All the odd numbered items are false and all the even numbered are true.

Although elderly people may become more limited physically, their intellects can increase with age—depending on their choices. Research suggests that many of the symptoms of senility have to do with overmedication or the wrong medication. Senility is no longer believed to be an inevitable development of old age. Physical stamina does slow down, but sexual relations continue into the decades of the seventies and eighties.

This brings to mind the story of a septugenarian couple at the doctor's office for their annual physical. All the tests were normal, and after pronouncing them in glowing good health, the doctor asked if anything were troubling them. The lady shyly replied, "Well, Doctor, we don't seem to be enjoying sex as much lately."

Suppressing his chuckle, the doctor asked, "When did you first notice this?"

The "old" lady replied, "Well, first last night, and then again this morning."

In order to feel less stress as the body grows older, it is helpful for aging people to change the pictures in their heads, so the differences between what they want and what they have will be reduced. B. F. Skinner wrote, "Old age is like fatigue, except that its effects cannot be corrected by relaxing or taking a vacation." Elderly people need to become realistic about what they can do each day and consider the limitations mind or body might be imposing on them.

I suggest that an efficient pathway for the elderly is to allow for more immediate reinforcement of needs than they may have allowed years before. Elderly people should take advantage of the time they have earned. In the past they may have waited and sacrificed for things, or perhaps they rushed vacations to work-imposed time limits.

I also recommend keeping familiar sources of need fulfillment around. Although many Senior Citizens have made choices to move into retirement communities or homes for the elderly, I am not sure that these are always the best pathways. If those who elect these alternate lifestyles have very good approaching skills and are extremely good at adjusting to new locations, then such choices may not cause undue stress. But for many aging people, changes in friends, location, and tearing up roots have negative consequences. A retirement community can be an isolated world where people are limited in exposure only to other senior citizens. This creates the illusion that aging is a painful and sad experience. In many homes for the elderly or retirement communities, conversation may be limited to ill health and the obituaries. The perception of aging as being a sad and painful experience can be offset by being part of the world where there are people of all ages, and where there is interaction among them.

Just in case the comments on aging feel as though they are hitting too close to home, I've included a fun checklist for you, so you can decide just how close you are to getting old:

YOU KNOW YOU'RE GETTING OLD WHEN . . .

Everything hurts and what doesn't hurt, doesn't work.
Your knees buckle, and your belt won't.
You sit down in a rocking chair and can't get it started.
You regret all those times you resisted temptation.
You order Geritol-on-the-rocks at the bar.
You think "gay" means "happy, lively, and vivacious."
You look forward to spending a quiet evening at home.

Your back goes out more often than you do.
You know all the answers, but nobody asks you the
   questions.
The last President you enjoyed voting for was Franklin
   Roosevelt.
You turned thirty-nine before Jack Benny.
Your little black book has only names ending in "M.D."
You need oxygen after blowing out your birthday candles.
Your mind makes agreements your body can't meet.
You finally get it all together and can't remember where
   you put it.
You start eating bran flakes and prune juice for breakfast.
You remember today that yesterday was your birthday.
You get worn out dialing long distance.
You buy a health club membership and don't go.
You have more hair on your chest than on your head.
You just can't seem to get around to procrastinating.
Your favorite newspaper column is *"Twenty-five years ago
   today."*
You don't need an alarm clock to get up at six in the
   morning.
You need a fire permit to light all the candles on your
   birthday cake.

Seriously, how close are you to old age? A few years away?
If your answer is "yes" or you are already there, then wel-
come to WhMPA-Land! Skill Builders recognize that getting
old is a process which begins at conception. Think about it!
John Holt, in *Escape From Childhood*, suggests that one of
the problems complicating life for children is the fact that
society has categorized them. Decades ago, kids were kids.
Now we have infants, toddlers, and so on until we reach ado-
lescence, which can also be subdivided into "pre" and
"post"! Once the label is applied, we treat accordingly.
Holt's idea extends to the elderly. We label and react as if we
were not in the process ourselves. There are unique develop-
mental differences for each age, however, the needs remain
the same. A child needs belonging and freedom just as an
older person does. **Health, regardless of chronological age,
means being in balance**. Unfortunately, adult children fre-

quently attempt to "take control" of their aging parent's health.

Such was the case of Barb, who came to me for help solving a problem with her seventy-four year old father. Barb, age forty-five, believed her father was not taking care of himself. I asked her to give me a specific example. It seemed there had been a lot of weddings in the family that year; the latest one triggered her visit to me. "Jennifer," a niece and the newest bride, celebrated the event with the typical reception for the small commumity—a huge dinner followed by drinking and dancing. Barb had watched her father as he ate, drank, and danced. Having a large family, Dad was going from one daughter or grandchild to another, dancing first a polka, then a waltz, following with the latest fad, disco. Barb's concern was the over-taxing of her father's heart. After a strenuous jitter-bug, she approached Dad and suggested she take him home. He refused the offer and continued to move on to the great-grandchildren. So Barb tried to enlist support from her mother and sister.

"Mom, Dad is really over-doing it. It's late besides. Don't you want to go home now?"

Mom laughed and said, "Oh, you know your Dad. He has such a good time, leave him alone! I'll go home with you though, because I'm tired and I want to help record the gifts tomorrow."

Barb approached her sister next. "Joan, I'm taking Mom home, but I do wish you'd get Dad to come or at least to stop dancing. He's going to die of a heart attack on the dance floor!"

"What better way for Dad to go—surrounded by those he loves, having fun and enjoying life!"

"I will pretend I didn't hear you say that!" Barb had experienced a major blowup with her sister over this incident, and now she was seeking my help to convince her father to change his lifestyle. Needless to say, Barb was a prime target for teaching the rethinking process—starting with what we can control.

As I listened to Barb's stories of her father, it was apparent that the old gentleman was quite healthy. All his needs were being met efficiently. He definitely was "in balance."

What can a well-meaning adult child do for her aging parents? She can demonstrate caring, ask questions, give alternatives, and model positive behaviors. What she cannot do is control her parents' lives. Time would be better spent educating herself about the aging process. Barb obviously loved her father and wanted him to live as long as possible. What she didn't realize was that only he could choose how to live his remaining years.

Numerous programs and activities exist for the elderly. It is a matter of exploring and choosing to get involved. Some, like Barb's father, do not seek organized functions. His lifestyle already incorporates balance. He takes daily walks in his small town, listening to the latest news, and stopping to talk with children and friends. Having owned a food store for many years, he now visits the old place to collect day-old bread and pastries which he distributes to the poor people on his walking route. Each day he listens to the radio to pick up new information as well as jokes. He loves to tell jokes!

Whether you are twenty or eighty, health is a process of finding a balance among and within your eight internal needs. If you want the lifestyle I believe produces a healthy body, you have only to rethink, then re-read all the need chapters. With this information stored in your brain, ask yourself, "Is what I am doing giving me enough of what I need?" If your answer is "no," you now have an alternative: the **Skill Building Process**.

PART III:
CONCLUSION

CHAPTER FIFTEEN

What Now? A Strategy for Change.

> "Everyone thinks of changing the
> world, but no one thinks of
> changing himself."
>
> Leo Tolstoy (on WhMPAs)

> "If it is to be, it is up to me."
>
> Skill Builder

It takes time to learn and apply the process of Skill Development. Remember, it took all your life to get where you are today. Try not to be impatient. Enjoy the thought that each day you change a little; now your changes can be planned to efficiently meet your needs.

By developing skills to change your perceptions, acting to achieve happiness won't be so difficult. By now, hopefully you know that is true. This doesn't mean there won't be times when it's easier to **wait** for the phone to ring, or that letter to come in the mail. There will also be days when you'll act to **change how others behave**. Using reward and/or punishment will work sometimes; other times you'll only be frustrated. A third choice to alter how you perceive the world is **substance abusing**. If you don't mind the after-effects, drinking and drugging are great choices for instant feel-good. All three choices inefficiently close the differences between what you need and what you have.

Now you have another choice. You can ask how much need fulfillment—happiness—you want, and proceed to learn a strategy that really works. That doesn't mean you have a magical formula or quick solution. What you do have is a process which begins with evaluating your present thinking. If you're too stressed, you can start the Skill Development method of rethinking. By planning each day to rethink what you have control over, what your needs are, what you choices are, what you can do to be fulfilled in all of your environments, and when things aren't right, what you can learn, you are gaining an edge for more happiness. You learn to perceive the glass as being **half full**.

The Skill Building Model is an exciting adventure when you acknowledge your achievements and practice the five steps.

When will you begin evaluating, rethinking, planning, acknowledging, and practicing? It's your choice. . . .

ABOUT THE AUTHOR

The staff members at the Center For Skill Development find it difficult to describe Dr. Applegate without resorting to such tired, worn-out adjectives as: "dedicated," "enthusiastic," "charismatic," and "caring." Less conventionally, Dr. Applegate is a refreshingly strong, positive, visible funmaker who enjoys learning and could stand to wash his car more often.

Born and raised in Southern California, Dr. Applegate completed his B.A. in Psychology at Loyola University, his M.A. at California University at Los Angeles, and his Ph.D. at Washington State University in 1969.

Throughout his life he has been influenced by many stimulating and loving people including his family, friends, and three other special individuals: John Hooper, his Boy Scout Leader, who taught him how to make friends; Father Joe Caldwell, his psychology teacher at Loyola University, who influenced his decision to study psychology; and Walt Disney, whom he met during his college days, and who helped him think beyond where most people are.

From 1969 to 1972 Dr. Applegate taught psychology at several universities and colleges in the Los Angeles area. Shortly after, he started his private practice and began to develop his strategy for teaching people how to build fulfilling successful lifestyles. Since 1975, over fifty thousand people have come to hear him speak at seminars and workshops throughout the United States.

In 1982 Dr. Applegate founded the Center For Skill Development, a not-for-profit organization designed to teach people thinking, acting, and feeling skills for their personal and professional lives. It is his hope that in the future others will not just teach Skill Building, but first live it.

A practicing Skill Builder himself, Dr. Applegate, who prefers to be called Gary, satisfies his need for fun through such hobbies as golf, tennis, gardening, and architecture. He works to maintain laughter and balance at his office in Sherman Oaks, California, and in his home in the hills of Los Angeles, where he lives with his wife, Suzanne.

YOU CAN ALWAYS WRITE TO GARY APPLEGATE

I am always willing to help. By my own philosophy, a helper is helping himself feel better.

Any message addressed to me and sent to the address below shall be given prompt and full attention.

CENTER FOR SKILL DEVELOPMENT
15335 Morrison Street, Suite 100
Sherman Oaks, California 91403

ABOUT THE CENTER FOR SKILL DEVELOPMENT

The Center is an organization with four primary divisions:

Mental Health
Business and Industry
Education
General Public

These four divisions are staffed by experienced, highly energetic professionals who teach the process of Skill Development in both individual and group settings. Some of the current programs and services offered through the Center include:

Certification Process

Training for individuals who want to learn and apply the concepts of Skill Development in their personal and professional lives. The process includes three two-day seminars: Life Skills, The Skill Development Teaching Model, and Professional Application. There are nine hours of practicum after each seminar. Certificates of competence are given upon completion.

Internship Program

This ongoing program fulfills the requirements for certification in Skill Development, and provides hours toward licensing in the State of California as a Marriage, Family, and Child Counselor and as a Clinical Psychologist.

Private Practice

C.S.D. offers private counseling for individuals with all forms of presenting problems. The Center specializes in dealing with difficult cases that have not been resolved in other settings.

Employee Assistance Program

An evaluation and referral service for business and industry is available through the Center, as well as a program to provide employees the skills necessary to be more effective on the job.

In-Service Program for Schools

This program teaches educators how to work together with a common approach to improve the delivery of educational services. Skill Development goes beyond traditional discipline methods (rules and consequences) and promotes permanent, rather than temporary change.

School Counseling

A program for counselors and school psychologists to learn a practical counseling model which is effective when working with students, teachers, parents, and administrators.

The Center presents seminars on Parenting, Relationships, Weight Control, Drugs and Alcohol, and other topics of general interest to people who want to improve their lives.

Tapes and Books

Instructional tapes are available for Mental Health, Relationships, Parenting, Personal Growth, and School In-service programs. For a specific list of tape topics and prices, or to order additional copies of *Happiness: It's Your Choice*, please contact the Center.

The above programs and services are offered in Los Angeles and at other locations throughout the year. If you are interested in setting up one or more of these programs in your area or facility, we will be happy to work with you in this process. We can be contacted at the following address:

CENTER FOR SKILL DEVELOPMENT
15335 Morrison Street, Suite 100
Sherman Oaks, California 91403

(818) 990-1700

INDEX

Outcome, fear of, 91
Parents
  as Skill Builders, 127–130
  worth 127–130
Passive vs. active, 125
Paying prices 55
  burning out, 52
  faith, 102
  fun, 187–204
  health, 217–234
  inefficient behaviors, 17
  knowledge, 217
  somatic paining, 51–52
  substance abusing, 55
Perceptions
  balance through, 28
  choice over input/output
    for freedom, 136
  controlling vs. other
    perceptions, 17
  interpretation of, 17,37
  rethinking through process,
    41–42
  substance abusing, 52
  WhMPA vs. Skill Builder
    meeting belonging needs,
    152
Plan 224
  eight criteria for good, 75
  routine and achievement, 75
  for sensory development, 75
  worth, 75
  see also Exercises and Needs;
    efficient behaviors
Poems
  To Laugh, 77
  You Know You're Getting
    Old When, 229
  Untitled, about goodbyes,
    160, 161
Power, 91
Powering in television
  relationships, 161
Process vs. outcome, 156
Procrastination, 137
Questions on Needs
  belonging, 150

faith, 98
freedom, 134
fun, 188
health, 218
knowledge, 206
security, 82
worth, 116
Quotations
  Allen, Woody (as WhMPA),
    97
  Applegate, Gary, 149
  Borge, Victor, 187
  Brenner, Dr. Paul, 217
  Bressler, Dr. David, 224
  da Vinci, Leonardo, 205
  Darwin, Charles, 15
  Einstein, Albert, 69
  Epictetus, 41
  Ford, Henry, 81
  Frank, Anne, 109
  Gunther, Bernard, 39
  Hastings, Robert J., 61
  Huxley, Thomas H., 115
  Jefferson, Thomas, 5
  Lewis, Thomas, 79
  Little Engine That Could,
    97
  Macleish, Archibald, 133
  Murphy's Law (as WhMPA),
    69
  Naisbett, John, 207
  Rolling Stones, 27
  Roosevelt, Eleanor, 91
  Runbeck, Margaret Lee 59
  Skill Builder, 235
  Skill Builder Elizabeth, 156
Quotations (continued)
  Skinner, B. F., 228–229
  Spanish Proverbs, 104, 105
  Tolstoy, Leo (on WhMPAs)
    235
Rejection, 79, 151, 154–155
Rethinking
  control, influence, 12, 17,
  defined, 17
  five areas related to power,
    207